D0898187

Failure Modes And Effects Analysis

Paul Palady

PT Publications, Inc.
Suite C
2273 Palm Beach Lakes Blvd.
West Palm Beach, FL 33409

Library of Congress Cataloging-in-Publication Data

Palady, Paul , 1950-
    Failure modes and effects analysis / Paul Palady.
                    p.   cm.
    Includes bibliographical references and index.
    ISBN 0-945456-17-4 (hard cover)
    1. Quality control. 2. Reliability (Engineering). I. Title.
    TS156.P23   1995
    658.5'62--dc20   95-36603
                                                                    CIP

To my son Brandon

Acknowledgements

We would like to thank the numerous companies and universities who have implemented FMEA techniques and sponsored seminars on the topic.

Corporations:

Acknowledgement to some of the corporations that have implemented FMEA technology: PPG, Teleflex, Lincoln Brass, Frigidaire, Eaton, Ford, Johnson & Johnson, General Motors, Tandem and Baxter.

Special thanks to:

Carl Garbe, Eaton - Aerospace

Fred Hooten, Food and Drug Administration

Carl Schwaighofer, Ethicon - Johnson & Johnson

Universities:

The University of Pittsburgh, Joseph M. Katz Graduate School of Business, Center for Executive Education (Regina L. Lewis)

The University of Wisconsin-Milwaukee, Center for Continuing Engineering Education (Terry Lynch and Roger Hirons)

Baldwin Wallace College Executive Seminars (Kay Corwin and Mary Jean Milanko)

Wayne State University, Department of Industrial and Manufacturing Engineering (Dr. Donald Falkenburg)

Preface

Is your organization currently doing FMEA, Failure Modes and Effects Analysis? If so, are you satisfied with the results? I have asked these two questions over the past several years to engineers, managers and technicians that have attend my seminar. The answer to the first question is mixed; however, the answer to the second question is overwhelmingly ... No! You are likely to get the same response if you were to asked this question in confidence to some of your coworkers. During a recent meeting, one manger, responsible for the corporate standards, questioned why I titled a SAE paper "Restoring The Effectiveness of FMEA," stating that this paper might imply that FMEA is not being used effectively in many cases. After some thought the manger certainly did not prefer this title but did agree that, in general, present applications in FMEA could be more effective.

The objective of this book is to restore FMEA as a vital development tool within the organization's quality and reliability programs. This objective will be accomplished by introducing new developments that 1) make FMEA accessible to more people in the organization, 2) improve the efficiency of constructing the FMEA and 3) increase the effectiveness of information extracted from the FMEA to make significant gains in quality and reliability. The first case study demonstrating these new developments was present in a paper (No. # 940884) at the SAE (Society of Automotive Engineers) International Congress in Detroit in 1994. It should be noted that these new developments in FMEA can provide significant benefits to all industries. Examples in the automotive industry, medical industry, food industry, as well as the service sector will be provided throughout this book. Some of these new developments

Failure Modes and Effects Analysis

introduced in the book may be in direct conflict with some of the traditional approaches to doing FMEA. (The graphic below illustrates these two approaches to FMEA.) I would ask that the reader, when comparing these new developments against the traditional approach, make comparisons from the customer's perspective and, more importantly, do an actual application. I am confident that the reader will realize the benefits associated to these new developments.

This book is dedicated to all the individuals in industry and the service sector who are directly accountable, stand behind and stand the closest to the day-to-day quality and reliability of their products and services.

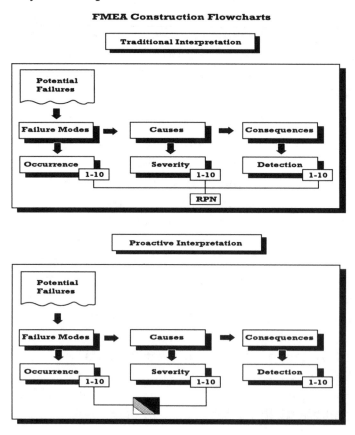

FMEA Construction Flowcharts

Chapter One:
FMEA Overview

What is an FMEA?

Failure Modes and Effects Analysis is a technique that provides three distinct functions:

1) FMEA is a *tool* for preventing problems.

2) FMEA is a *procedure* for developing and implementing new or revised designs, processes or services.

3) FMEA is the *diary* of the design, process or service.

As a tool, FMEA is one of the most effective low-risk techniques for predicting problems and identifying the most cost-effective solutions for preventing these problems. As a procedure, FMEA provides a structured approach for evaluating, tracking and updating design and process developments for all disciplines within the organization. It can be used to link and maintain many of the other documents of the organization. As a diary, FMEA is initiated at the conception of the design, process or service and is maintained throughout the saleable life of the product. All changes that occur during this time that affect the quality or the reliability of the product must be assessed and documented in the FMEA. Each of these three functions of FMEA will be expanded upon using examples in subsequent sections of this book.

How does FMEA work?

This tool is most effective when applied as a team effort; however, FMEA can be and has been implemented as an individual effort. The advantages and the disadvantages of each approach can be assessed by weighing the cost and the benefits associated with each approach.

Failure Modes and Effects Analysis

The development and the implementation of FMEA adds cost; however, when *done effectively*, it can result in significant quality and reliability payback. This payback is realized by reducing the failure cost by pooling the collective subject matter knowledge of everyone (the team) who understands how the design, process, or service is 1) designed 2) manufactured and 3) used and misused. When the FMEA is done as a team, the chance of identifying and preventing more of the potential failure modes is much higher than that of a one individual. While the cost of developing an FMEA is much lower for one individual, the chances of identifying and preventing more of the potential failure modes is considerably less and the resulting quality/reliability payback may not exceed the cost of developing and maintaining the FMEA.

One person doing his/her best cannot be as effective as a team working together.

As mentioned, Failure Modes and Effects Analysis should be developed and implemented by a team. One of the objectives of the team is to support the design responsible engineer. FMEA *is not* designed to supersede the engineer's judgment or work. It is simply a tool to assist the engineer in identifying more of the potential problems that he/she may have not considered. The engineer is likely to possess the most knowledge of the design; however, as one person, he/she cannot see this design as other disciplines see it. Being able to look at the design from all perspectives is one of the advantages of doing FMEA as a team. Every discipline or group that influences the final design quality/ reliability or that will be affected by the design may be able to provide additional insight for identifying potential problems and assist in preventing these potential problems.

You do not have to create a problem before you can fix it.

It is important to note that the FMEA is proactive, implying that potential problems will be eliminated before they have actually been created on a prototype, during the process or in the field. The most common question is, How can you fix the problem unless you have seen it or experienced it? FMEA is highly subjective and requires considerable guess work on what could happen and how to prevent it. This guessing is done by the subject matter experts who have accumulated intimate experience with the design, process or service. Often the team can draw on historical performance data from previous generations of the design to assist in identifying some of the potential failure modes, the consequences of these potential failure modes and the causes attributed to these potential failure modes. If this data is not available or the revisions for the new design generation are so drastic that any historical data cannot be used, the team must rely completely on their knowledge and expertise of the subject matter. This is one reason why the selection of the FMEA team and the subsequent planning of the FMEA are important elements in the overall FMEA project. Details on team selection and FMEA planning are presented in the following section titled "Prerequisites to FMEA."

Types of FMEAs

Two distinct types of FMEA have emerged since its development in the mid-sixties: 1) the design FMEA (DFMEA) and 2) the process FMEA (PFMEA). Within these two types, several versions and variations of FMEA and the FMEA forms have surfaced. They share the same objectives and require common basic elements to achieve these objectives. These different versions and the variations in the forms are reviewed in the subsequent section titled "FMEA Interpretation."

The distinction between the design FMEA and the process FMEA lies in the objectives. Each type has two very different objectives and these two objectives can best be realized in the form of two questions: For the design FMEA, the team asks the questions:

◊ How can this *design* fail to do what it is suppose to do?

◊ What should we do to prevent these potential *design* failures?

For the process FMEA, the team asks a different question:

◊ How can this *process* fail to do what it is suppose to do?

◊ What should we do to prevent these potential *process* failures?

These are two very different objectives that must be pursued in separate FMEAs to avoid compromising the design objectives over the process objectives and vice versa. I believe that the engineering and manufacturing communities both agree on this one, that no additional help is needed in this area of compromise! It is also important to acknowledge that the design and the process both exert influence on one another. Some of the failure modes from the design may be caused by actions during the process and some process failure modes may be caused by the design. Regardless of where the cause is generated, it must be addressed before a failure mode in either of these FMEA can be prevented. Some of the existing workbooks on FMEA suggest that all potential design problems must be resolved with design actions. This restricts problem prevention and reduces the efficiency and effectiveness of prevention. This will be explained in detailed and demonstrated with examples in the section on "FMEA Interpretation." If a potential design problem can be prevented more efficiently and effectively by a process action or vice versa, then it should be considered.

> *"Follow the least cost, and the straightest path toward problem prevention."*
> — H. Bajaria, R. Copp, SPS, 1991

Preventing design problems with a manufacturing action in some cases may be the least costly and the straightest path. This is referred to as "forgiving downstream" or the Forgiving Principle. Preventing process problems with a design action may, in other instances, be the most efficient and effective strategy. This is referred to as "controlling upstream." The FMEA team should consider both options when analyzing the FMEA.

Other types of analysis very similar to FMEA have been used to identify potential problems and to identify the appropriate corrective action. These type of analysis are often referred to as: Hazard Analysis; Fault Hazard Analysis (FHA); Criticality Analysis (CrA); Risk Analysis; or Failure Modes, Effects and Criticality Analysis (FMECA). These are some of the more common names or acronyms. It should be noted that many sectors of industry have some formal procedure for assessing potential problems and identifying the appropriate corrective actions toward prevention. In fact all organizations will say that this is an assumed part of the employees job. However, these industry specific procedures may not be identified by one of the above acronyms. New developments in FMEA, introduced in this book, will increase the efficiency and the effectiveness of this key job element which is part of every employee's job description!

Basic elements of all FMEAs

All of the variations of FMEA must include five basic elements to guarantee their effectiveness or their success. Should any of the elements shown in Figure 1.1 be excluded, the contribution the FMEA will have on final quality/reliability is likely to be very small, if any at all. In other words, the initial investment in developing the FMEA may not result in an return on investment in the form of failure cost reduction.

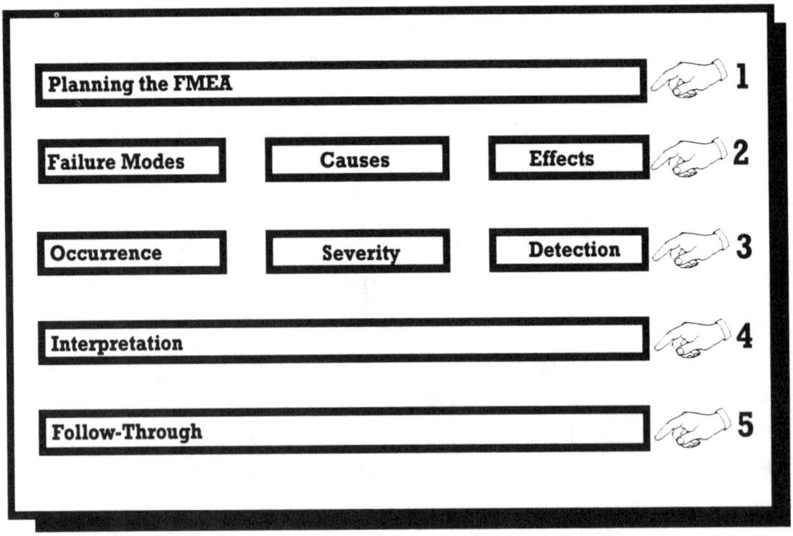

Planning the FMEA			1
Failure Modes	Causes	Effects	2
Occurrence	Severity	Detection	3
Interpretation			4
Follow-Through			5

Figure 1.1

The five elements from Figure 1.1 are defined below:

1) Selecting the FMEA project that has the greatest potential for quality and reliability payback for the organization and its customers.

2) Asking and answering the following three questions:

    ◊ How could it fail?

    ◊ Why does it fail?

    ◊ What happens when it fails?

3) Implementing a scheme for extracting the most important failure modes to work on or improve. Typically, the most common scheme is to quantify and rank each of these three categories. There are two approaches for this element of the FMEA and it can create confusion. One approach is to rate the occurrence and the detection of each cause contributing to the failure mode. The other approach is to rate the occurrence and the detection of the failure mode. Regardless of approach used by the FMEA team, the conclusions should be the same. This will be demonstrated using an example in the section on "FMEA Interpretation."

4) Prioritizing or selecting the potential failure modes to work on first. The traditional approach employed the Risk Priority Number, RPN, or the Criticality Number, Cr, for prioritizing the failure modes. The RPN number can be misleading. This will be demonstrated using examples later in the book, as well as a new approach for prioritizing the failure modes to assist the reader in deciding which

approach best fits the needs of his/her organization.

Beware of the problem solver who only owns one tool.

5) The last element is the Follow-Through. The construction and the analysis of the FMEA are likely to require application of other supporting quality and reliability tools. Often data must be analyzed using statistical methods before one of the FMEA columns can be completed or recommendations can be approved for corrective action. If the ability to apply these supporting tools or the commitment for follow-through is lacking within the team, very little or no benefits can be expected from this FMEA other than being able to produce a form for the audit.

FMEA as a universal quality program requirement

As mentioned, FMEA is a requirement for all organizations and quality standards. Some organizations or standards do not specifically refer to it as FMEA or other acronym. However, they all require the employees and suppliers to make a genuine effort to anticipate potential problems and implement the best options available for preventing or controlling these potential failure modes. As previously mentioned, this is part of the engineer's thought process when designing or revising a product, process or service. This is FMEA.

All companies agree that the risk of introducing a new design or design change must be completely assessed; however, many organizations and some quality standards have yet to specifically name FMEA as a technique for doing so. It is anticipated that FMEA will be a universal requirement for organizations and quality standards in the near future. Currently, some organizations have FMEA as a requirement of their quality programs for the organizations and their suppliers. Some examples include the new joint automotive (Chrysler/Ford/General Motors) quality standard Quality System QS-9000 and the Department of Defense Military Standard 1629A (currently under revision). FMEA is being considered for quality standards that serve as guidelines, although not requirements, for other industry sectors, such as the Food and Drug Administration's cGMP (current Good Manufacturing Practices) and the International Organization for Standards quality series, ISO 9000 standards.

Measurable benefits of FMEA

Remember, FMEA requires an initial cost by the organization. This includes the team member's time and, one of the more expensive activities, meetings. This initial cost can be an investment providing that the FMEA is done effectively. This return on investment will be realized by the customer, as well as the organization, in the form of reduced failure cost. This concept is depicted in Figure 1.2. Reduced failure cost as depicted in Figure 1.2 results in higher dividends. Organizations can assign all expenditures associated to the business in one of the following three categories:

1) Prevention Cost

2) Appraisal Cost

3) Failure Cost

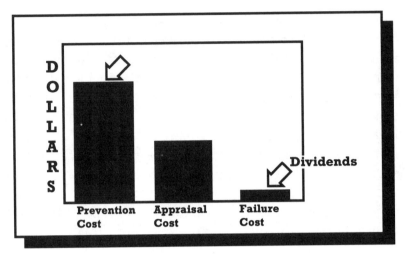

Figure 1.2

Developing and maintaining FMEAs is a prevention cost. An organization that invests in this category may or may not realize a substantial return on investment. This will depend on how effectively the prevention tools are implemented, which requires a sound practical understanding of these tools. Figure 1.3 represents an example of three possible scenarios that reflect an organization's total cost.

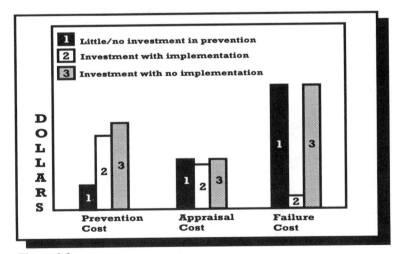

Figure 1.3

◊   The number **"1"** bars represent an organization with little investment in prevention being forced to allocate much of its cash flow into the failure cost category.

◊   The number **"2"** bars represent an organization investing in prevention with a substantial returns through the reduction of its failure cost.

◊   The number **"3"** bars represent an organization investing heavily in prevention training, unfortunately, without effective implementation.

The appraisal cost is associated with an activity that all organizations must conduct periodically to assure that corrective actions that were established for assuring the designed-in quality and reliability continue to work and are still effective for accomplishing these quality and reliability goals. These activities are commonly referred to as audits, follow-up surveys and final inspection. Examples of some prevention cost tools or activities in addition to the FMEA include: Quality Function Deployment (QFD), reliability planning, fault tree analysis (FTA), preaward surveys, design of experiments, Taguchi Methods/Robust Design, Statistical Problem Prevention, tolerance design and statistical tolerancing. Some example of failure costs include: engineering changes based on failures that have occurred, additional costs due to poor planning, sorting, scrap, rework and all other cost initiated by a failure including some of the more costly, lasting, and damaging failures such as customer dissatisfaction, company reputation and market share loss.

Failure Modes and Effects Analysis

Exercise 1a (Quality Cost)

For example, plant Z has caused a temporary line shut down at its sister assembly plant D because it has shipped components that were out of specification and could not be assembled. The sister plant had to temporarily shut down the line and implement one hundred percent inspection and sorting until plant Z could ship acceptable components. Plant Z also agreed to check its existing inventory before shipping any more of these components. They also agreed to air freight all of the good components that they had.

The corporate office recommends sending some of the quality engineers to explain this situation to the Original Equipment Manufactures. All agree that after these interim actions have been put in place a task force should be developed to study how this problem can be preventing from occurring in the future.

◊   Identify all the activities.

◊   Place each activity in the appropriate cost category.

◊   Where are most of the resources being consumed?

◊   What conclusions can you draw?

Answer to exercise 1a is in the appendix.

If this exercise sounds familiar, it is purely coincidental.

Some of the benefits from developing and maintaining effective FMEAs are summarized below:

◊　Saves on development costs & time

◊　Serves as a guide for more efficient test planning

◊　Assists in the development of cost-effective preventive maintenance systems

◊　Provides insight for designing built-in test

◊　Minimizes unforeseen events when planning a process

◊　Provides a quick reference for problem solving

◊　Reduces engineering changes

◊　Improves customer satisfaction

◊　Serves as a key for tracking the design and providing updates through the organization

◊　Minimizes unnecessary costly controls in the process

◊　Identifies safety concerns to be addressed

◊　Provides insight for Robust Design against customer habits

◊　Safeguards against repeating the same mistakes in the future

◊　Captures and retains product and process knowledge for the organization

◊　Saves on development costs & time:

Many of the development programs that I have participated in and observed have sacrificed much of the initial planning time for advancing the prototype development.

These prototypes are quickly tested and subsequent test failures identified on the prototypes. This strategy is referred to as "find-and-fix." This cycle of find-and-fix often continues well into the start of the production phase and may extend into the manufacturing operation and out to the final customers. One example is the comparison of the design development cycle for U.S. industry against some of the companies in Japan. This comparison depicts Japanese companies spending much more time in the planning phase and finishing with much less failure cost for manufacturing start up and overall higher quality for the customer.

Unlike the Japanese companies, most U.S. companies do not spend considerable time in planning stages of design development. Instead, these companies continue to find and fix problems in the prototypes, an expensive, time-consuming practice. The result is a higher failure cost for manufacturing and a lower level of quality.

A comparison of the costs associated with each of these find-and-fix applications can be made by developing an effective FMEA and tracking all the associated development and manufacturing launch costs. These costs can then be compared to a similar program where FMEA was not used or the strategy of find-and-fix was applied to the prototypes. This comparison should reveal a significant difference in the failure cost and development time.

◊ Serves as a guide to more efficient test planning:

The chapter titled "FMEA Linkage" provides examples on how the information developed from the FMEA provide input to test planning and how the results of the test can influence future development for FMEA. Basically, the FMEA provides the test planners with greater confidence that all tests truly reflect the design performance and that no unnecessary tests are preformed.

◊   Assists in the development of preventative maintenance systems:

If it ain't broke; don't fix it ... sometimes!

Do you agree with the statement above? Most people outside the maintenance profession tend to strongly disagree with this statement, but actually practice this! For example scheduled preventative maintenance can be very expensive and sometimes may outweigh the benefits. A majority of car owners are likely to practice this philosophy with some of the items listed in their vehicle maintenance schedule booklet. With items such as oil changes and engine coolant changes, the schedules are rigidly adhered to. The severity of these failure modes will register very high in the FMEA. With other items, such as inspecting the exhaust heat shield or inspecting and cleaning the windshield wiper blades, the owners decide to wait until they break before they fix them. These owners have made a conscious decision that the cost of preventive maintenance on these items far exceed the benefits in time and money of any quality or reliability benefits that could be gained by investing in preventative maintenance. Studies from one tire manufacture have shown that in some cases the cost to rotate the tires on some vehicles exceeds any benefits that could be realized by extending the life of the tires with no adverse effect in the performance of these tires. The FMEA will provide greater assurance that resources are allocated for preventative maintenance only where required. Failure modes in the FMEA that have low severity numbers and low occurrence numbers may not justify an expensive preventative maintenance schedule.

Failure Modes and Effects Analysis

◊   Provides insight for designing built-in test:

While, built-in test (BIT) may be required for some complex systems, it adds to the cost of the design. The FMEA provides insight to the necessity of the BIT based on the severity number, the detection number and the description of the effects.

◊   Minimizes unforeseen events when planning a process:

Similar to the strategy of substituting find-and-fix in the FMEA with find-and-fix on the prototypes, find-and-fix during manufacturing can also be substituted for find-and-fix in the process flow diagram using process FMEA. The reader is asked to recall past experience of launching a new design or confer with a senior colleague that may be able to exchange some experience in this area. I am confident that many will agree process FMEA will provide benefits for process planning.

◊   Provides a quick reference for problem solving:

The FMEA can be used to quickly identify the source of special cause problems that sometimes occur during production or out in the field. It is possible that information contained in the cause column or the recommendation column of the FMEA can quickly pinpoint the problem and direct the problem-solving team toward the solution. New solutions identified during the problem solving should be used to update the FMEA.

◊   Reduces engineering changes:

It may not be possible to completely eliminate the need for engineering changes within the organization; however, some of these changes can be eliminated with the development of an effective FMEA. Again changing the design in the FMEA form requires a fraction of the time and money that would be required to make these changes on the parts, during manufacturing and out in the field. This is one of the fundamental elements of making better designs in less time!

◊   Improves customer satisfaction:

The FMEA is a tool designed primarily for preventing problems before they occur. Once a problem has occurred, failure cost has been generated and much of this failure cost is transferred to the customer and eventually finds its way back to the organization in the form of lost sales. This can be measured using Dr. Genichi Taguchi's Loss Function. This failure cost can eventually result in a more personal cost such as reductions in head count.

Designing-in systems that provide faster responses to problems may improve customer satisfaction to a small degree. Regardless how responsive the organization is to its failures, it is important to recognize that failure costs have been generated for the customer!

◊   Serves as a key for tracking the design and providing updates through the organization:

All new designs or proposed changes should be initially evaluated in the FMEA. The FMEA is the logical starting point or the lead document for all changes or revisions made to the design, process or service. Many of these revisions are likely to cause revisions in other documentation or procedures in other departments of the organization. The heading of the FMEA can be designed to include a checklist of all documentation that can be influenced by revisions initialed in the FMEA. For example information from the FMEA can affect 1) test plans, 2) process flow diagrams, 3) block diagrams, 4) manufacturing control plans and even the 5) quality contracts of the purchase agreement, as well as the design prints. Examples of how the FMEA influence other activities within the organization are presented in the "FMEA Linkage" section of this book.

◊   Minimizes unnecessary costly controls in production:

Information extracted from both the design FMEA and the process FMEA can help the process planners identify, with greater confidence, which process controls are required and which controls are not necessary. The FMEAs can also provide insight on locating the optimum points to place these controls in the process, process control points. These controls should be considered only after sufficient reduction in both the severity and occurrence numbers in the FMEA are not attainable.

◊   Identifies safety concerns to be address:

High severity numbers in the FMEA are an indication that the corresponding failure mode is likely to produce effects that will jeopardize the customer's safety. When establishing the FMEA procedures, the degree of safety risk can be defined and the appropriate severity numbers assigned to each definition of risk for the customer. Special requirements can be established for failure modes that can produce severity numbers that exceed a specified number.

◊   Provides insight for Robust Design against customer habits:

The Robust Design concept has recently arrived at the

forefront of the quality and the reliability programs. Robust Design simply means designing a product that is insensitive to the variation that this product will be exposed to during the its life. Some examples of the variation that the design should be robust against include: the environment, customer habits and uncontrolled variation from the manufacturing process. Uncontrolled variation is often referred to as noise, not to be confused with sound noise. These sources of uncontrolled variation are often identified very early in the FMEA, eliminating surprises in manufacturing and surprises for the final customers.

When this noise exerts significant influence on the design, to the extent that it will completely distort the engineer's model or performance predictions, the engineer must try to minimize the effects of this variation by designing-in features that will desensitize the design to these sources of uncontrolled variation or noise.

Words of caution

Some of the common obstacles encountered and common misapplication of FMEA are:

◊   FMEA is not designed to supersede the engineer's work.

◊   Every conceivable failure mode should not be evaluated in the FMEA.

◊   FMEA is not the tool for selecting the optimum design concept.

◊   FMEA, as do all tools, has limitations. Additions to the FMEA form are likely to distract from the primary FMEA objective.

◊   The Severity, Occurrence and Detection Scales

should be tailored to reflect the organization's products and processes.

◊ If your are not sure what number to assign to any of the ranking scales, don't assign the highest number.

◊ The RPN, Risk Priority Number, can be misleading.

◊ Applying the Pareto principle to the RPN is a misapplication of the Pareto principle.

◊ Very small RPN may justify corrective action.

◊ The majority of the FMEA should not be developed in a meeting.

◊ FMEA team members that are located in other buildings, cities, states and countries must participate in the FMEA. This can be done cost-effectively using the new developments in FMEA presented in the case study (SAE Paper #940884, Palady/Horvath/Thomas, 1994).

Each of the above items will be demonstrated in detail using examples throughout the book; however, for this overview section only brief paragraphs of each item will be provided.

The engineer's knowledge of the physics of the design or process, along with the his/her experience and intuition, supersedes all statistical, quality and reliability analysis. The sciences play a supporting role to assist the engineer in making decisions; not to dictate the decisions! It should be acceptable for the engineer to dismiss data that is in conflict with the physics of the design or the past experience. However, it is not valid for the engineer to dismiss data simply because it does not agree with the preferable answer.

Only the failure modes that are real issues should be considered for a complete evaluation in the FMEA. For example, consider including all the conceivable failure modes of one major component of an automobile or equipment. Investigating all of the conceivable failure modes can easily exceed the available resources of any budget. The FMEA team, which includes all the experts that understand how the product is designed, manufactured, stored, shipped, used and misused, will be able to identify all the legitimate failure modes that should be entered into the FMEA form.

FMEA can be used to select the optimum design or process concept; however, it is a very expensive approach. A less expensive tool that can be just as effective is Concept Selection (Pugh). When using the statistical, quality and reliability tools there are many ways to arrive at the answer. As in any profession, the skill is in getting the answer using the fastest less expensive tool.

FMEA, as with most tools, can be modified to accept other types of information and extended to perform additional analysis in the name of continuous improvement. Applying the "Swiss Army Knife" approach or additional tasks to the FMEA form is likely to introduce more confusion and opportunities for misapplication.

Adopting or directly transferring rating scales from FMEA training manuals of generic guidelines is likely to increase the time required to development FMEAs. If the definitions for the rating numbers are vague or do not reflect the organization's quality history and strategies for process control this will encourage unnecessary debate and confusion when assigning rating numbers.

Failure Modes and Effects Analysis

If you are not sure of the number to assign when rating the severity, occurrence or detection do not guess high. The argument behind the "guessing high" strategy is the mistakes will be made on the conservative side. Errors in any direction incur cost to the organization, as well as the final customers. If a team member is not sure, this member should abstain from voting. If all team members disagree, they should pursue one of the statistical tools that are designed for determining the relationship between the rating number and the subject being rated. The Risk Priority Number is the product of three scales; two of these scales are proactive, the other reactive. Allocating resources for improvement or making decisions based on the RPN may result in little or no improvement to the problem. Examples are provide in the section on "FMEA Interpretation." Applying the Pareto Principle to the RPNs is a misapplication of the Pareto Principle.

Failure modes E, F and G, shown in Figure 1.4, may result in more severe consequences or occur at a higher frequency than failure mode A or B. If this is the case than failure modes E, F and G should be addressed first. Since the RPN is a product of three scales, the RPN of A and B can be artificially inflated by a high detection number but have less severe consequences than a failure mode with a lower RPN. Therefore, calculating the RPN and applying the Pareto principle to the RPNs allows opportunity for distraction from some of the more important failure modes. Detailed discussion and examples are provide in the section on FMEA interpretation.

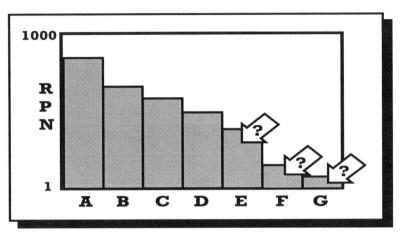

Figure 1.4

On occasion the FMEA team may elect not to investigate Risk Priority Numbers that are below a certain value in the effort to save time and other resources. This thinking is certain to eventually cause the FMEA team to overlook a critical failure mode that has been documented in the FMEA! It should be noted that the answers are not contained in the RPN. They are found in the three individual numbers that are used to calculate the RPN.

FMEA does not require large amounts of meeting time or excessive blocks of time to sequester the team in a room to develop the FMEA. FMEA can be and is developed cost effectively and more efficiently as a team effort when less time is spent in meetings. New developments will be introduced demonstrating how this is possible

Failure Modes and Effects Analysis

Summary

This book takes a detailed look at the problems limiting the effectiveness of FMEA in industry today and provides suggestions and new developments for restoring the effectiveness of FMEA as the primary tool in the development process.

FMEA is: 1) A tool for preventing problems, 2) an efficient approach for coordinating and updating new developments or incorporating revisions and 3) the diary for the design, process or service.

FMEA is a team tool used to assist the engineer; it is not designed to evaluate the engineer's work or supersede the engineer's decision making.

FMEA can be divided into two distinct categories: design FMEA (DFMEA) and process FMEA (PFMEA). They must be developed separately to avoid prematurely compromising the objectives. Each category has separate objective; however, it is important to understand the causes in the DFMEA influence the PFMEA and vice versa. Decisions made based on the interpretation of either FMEA may introduce changes to the other FMEA.

All organizations are actively involved in FMEA. Some have very formal procedures and clear policies while other organizations intuitively apply FMEA inductive thinking when developing or revising a design, process or service.

Five basic elements included in all effective FMEAs are: 1) FMEA planning 2) brainstorming the failure modes, the causes and the effects 3) prioritizing and extracting the most important failure modes 4) interpreting or reading the results and 5) following through in the actions required to develop an effective FMEA and on the recommendations suggested in the FMEA.

FMEA is specified as a requirement for the Chrysler/ Ford/GM new QS-9000, the Department of Defense Military Standard 1629A, and in other industries. Identifying potential problems and implementing preventative action is an implied requirement for every organization and all other quality standards, such as ISO 9000 and TQM. It is very likely that FMEA will be recommended for other sectors of industry, such as the medical and service providers.

Developing and maintaining FMEA require time and money. The payback from this investment is expected to be substantial for the customer and the organization in terms of failure cost reduction.

Note The RPN can be misleading in the interpretation of FMEA. New developments are introduced that convert this traditional interpretation to a completely proactive interpretation.

Some questions to be considered prior to FMEA implementation:

◊ How to gain the engineer's approval and support?

◊ Should the team study every conceivable failure mode?

◊ Should FMEA be use to select the concept?

◊ Should the rating scales be tailored for our FMEAs?

◊ Should we make decisions based on the RPN?

◊ How can we measure the cost/benefits of FMEA?

Chapter Two: Prerequisites to FMEA

Planning the FMEA

One of the most common mistakes in the implementation of FMEA is the lack of planning. Most often the team decides to begin constructing the FMEA form immediately, listing the most obvious function, the failure modes, and the subsequent effects of the failure modes and attempting to proceed right through to the recommended actions. This approach can create confusion, add unnecessary cost and limit the usefulness of the completed FMEA.

It is likely that those with hands-on experience in FMEA applications will be able to identify, firsthand, with some of the problems that are attributed to developing FMEAs without planning them. Many of these problems surface in the form of questions or encourage lengthy discussion such as:

◊   Who should be responsible for the FMEA?

◊   Who should participate and how should they participate?

◊   Should we assess the system, the subsystem or the individual components (top down) or should we start with the components (bottom up)?

◊   When should we begin the FMEA?

◊   Can we start the Process FMEA during the development of the Design FMEA?

◊   Should we consider this as a failure mode?

◊   Is this the failure mode, is it the effect or is it the cause?

◊   Should we rate the occurrence and the detection of the failure mode or should we rate the occurrence and the detection of the cause?

◊ What rating should we assign to the scales?

◊ How can we efficiently and accurately assign numbers when the team is in disagreement?

◊ Should we construct the FMEA by assessing each failure mode from left to right or is there any advantage to constructing each column in its entirety before proceeding to the next sequential column?

◊ Are we doing this correctly?

All of these questions can be addressed in the planning phase of FMEA. Some are specific to establishing the FMEA guidelines and suggestions for preserving team dynamics for FMEA. The time spent in this phase will get the team off to a slower start; however, the odds of a strong finish will be in the team's favor. In addition to completing the FMEA on schedule and within budget, the effectiveness of the FMEA will improve significantly. Without any efforts to plan the FMEA, there is a high probability of not finishing the FMEA as a team and the benefits are questionable.

Who should be responsible for the FMEA? Often the organization attempts to distribute the responsibility equally to the team. This does not fit our culture! A group of individuals simply cannot take responsibility for a project easily. This is proven on a daily basis, at the first sign of problems the team members are likely to volunteer or offer up each others help. This theory can easily be tested next time you encounter a problem involving a team and attempt to resolve it via the telephone. All FMEAs must be assigned to one individual. This person will be responsible for the FMEA timing, the budget and most of all the effectiveness of the FMEA. (Ref. Theory Z Management by W. Ouchi)

One person does not posses all the answers.

Who should develop the FMEA? One common misconception is that the person responsible for the FMEA is the person who should develop the FMEA. The FMEA must be developed by a team, not developed by an individual. One person on the team (the engineer) is likely to possess the bulk of the knowledge of the subject matter; however, as an individual this person cannot clearly see and understand everything about that design, process or service. Not knowing everything should not be viewed as being incapable or not competent; otherwise, all the honest people will fall in this category. This brings us to the fundamental objective of FMEA that I believe has been lost over the years: FMEA is designed to catch the small percentage of potential problems that the engineer has not considered. It was *not designed* to replicate the engineer's work.

The engineer or the person most knowledgeable about the subject matter may possess eighty, ninety or ninety-five percent of the answers or predictions of the potential problems. However, we cannot be content with resolving anything less than one hundred percent. One hundred percent or a reliability of (1) may not be attainable in the long run, but we must continue to strive closer to this ideal target. FMEA is the tool for assisting the engineer in preventing as many potential problems as possible within the resource limitations of the organization. Again, the ideal is preventing one hundred percent.

Two essential tasks in planning the FMEA are 1) the selection of the person responsible for the development and the maintenance of the FMEA and 2) the selection of the other individuals that will make up the FMEA team. These individuals must be capable of completing assignment requirements of the FMEA and willing to accept the assignments delegated by the FMEA manager or person responsible. The FMEA manager should be the engineer or an individual responsible for the design, process or service. The reason for this is best explained by an analogy. The best chance of bring up well-adjusted children of the highest possible quality is when the individuals responsible for the design concept also takes responsibility of the subsequent development!

Another question that must be resolved in the planning phase is, Should we develop "top-down" FMEAs or should we develop "bottom-up" FMEAs? A top-down FMEA defines the approach for beginning the analysis at the system level then proceeding to the subsystem level and then down to the individual components. For this approach the team is likely to develop one system FMEAs, a few subsystem FMEAs and many component FMEAs. The top-down strategy may not be practical for large complex systems.

The bottom-up approach to FMEA, as suggested, begins with the development of the individual component FMEAs, these FMEAs serve as input to the subsystem FMEAs and eventually feed into or are combined to assist in the development the system FMEA.

Some considerations for selecting the top-down or the bottom-up approach for developing FMEAs are:

◊ Program timing

◊ Program cost

◊ Availability of personnel

For example, one reliability program established a top-down policy for the development of FMEA. After reviewing the program timing and the program budget the project manager revised the top-down approach to include only a system FMEA and component FMEAs, excluding subsystem FMEAs. After notification that the design responsible engineer for the system would not be in the country for the first six week of the start of the program (joint overseas program), the project manager elected to begin with developing the component FMEAs. Each of the component engineers were required to develop the component FMEA in concert with the respective suppliers. The component FMEAs were referenced during the development of the system FMEA which was developed on schedule and within budget.

The FMEA planning team must agree on when to initiate the development of the FMEA. FMEA should follow the identification of the requirements and the selection of the preliminary concept. This does not suggest that the functional specifications and design prints must be developed to the approval stage. It does suggest that the requirements and the concept should be agreed upon before any work begins on the FMEAs. FMEA can be used to identify requirements and for selecting the best concept; however, other tools can accomplish these tasks much more accurately and efficiently. For example, Quality Function Deployment (QFD) can be used to minimize the risk for identifying the requirement or function, and concept selection can be used to select the concept that can best satisfy the requirements. For example, one company elected to begin a new design development program without any of the planning activities suggested. The rational was that *"the sooner we begin ... the sooner we will finish."* Several weeks into the preliminary concept phase of the program a decision was made by top management to develop and build a radically different concept based on market research that was available at the start of the program but not linked to the FMEA. Approximately several thousand dollars in man-hours, travel time and meetings were spent on the FMEA; unfortunately, the information from this FMEA could not be transferred or provide any input to the develop of the FMEAs for the new concept. To conserve program resources the FMEA development team should consider 1) minimizing the risk for identifying the design/process functions using the first chart of QFD and 2) selecting and agreeing on the basic concept.

One other frequently asked question is, Should we do FMEA on an existing design where no changes are being considered? This depends on the quality/reliability return on investment potential. Of all the existing designs being manufactured by the organization, which of them have the greatest opportunities for quality/reliability improvement? In other words, what designs are causing the most problems, and are some of these generating a higher failure cost than anticipated from the introduction of the new designs? Simply stated, do FMEA where you need it the most!

The planning group must also decide when to start the process FMEA. Again this will depend on the program timing, the budget and the availability of the team. The process FMEA (PFMEA) should begin as soon as possible (following the design concept and process concept). It is important to recognize that information extracted from the PFMEA can influence the development of the design FMEA and vice versa.

The FMEA ground rules

To ensure effective and efficient FMEAs, ground rules must be established, understood and agreed upon in the planning phase. Suggestions for the ground rules are presented below:

Ground Rule 1. Do not consider all conceivable failure modes.

This is likely to generate a strong reaction; however, let's look at the practical side of this statement. Looking at all the conceivable failure modes will certainly add to the analysis, cost and timing without any real benefit.

Should the team agree that a failure mode is physically possible but that this failure mode is not practical, this failure should not enter into the FMEA form. As mentioned, the team is made up of the subject matter "experts," those most knowledgeable about how the product is designed, manufactured, used and misused. On the other hand, if one of the team members insists on entering this failure mode into the FMEA form, it should be entered to preserve team dynamics. If this failure mode is indeed unimportant it will become obvious as the team progresses through the FMEA. Recall, FMEA requires 1) subject matter knowledge from all aspects of the design life 2) a working level understanding of the quality and reliability tools and 3) a healthy dose of common sense.

Ground Rule 2. Write the failure mode as the negative of the function.

As the team begins to list the failure modes, questions will arise as to whether this failure mode is really an effect or possible a cause. For example, a leak could be identified as a failure mode for many designs. If this is applied to the reader's specific example an argument may be made that this leak could be the effect or it could be the cause. This will encourage plenty of discussion. Should the team find itself unable to decide on how to identify the failure mode or that the discussion on this failure mode is consuming too much of the allocated FMEA time, they can establish a ground rule: *write the failure mode as the function in the negative sense.* For example, if one of the functions of the design is "to contain the liquid or the gas" then the failure mode of this function described in the negative sense is "it will not contain the liquid or the gas." This ground rule is simple and it works!

Ground Rule 3. Select an approach for rating the failure modes or causes.

Another ground rule should be established to resolve some confusion that has been introduced with the evolution of the FMEA forms. The earlier versions of the forms located the three scales occurrence, severity and detection together and on the right side of the form. The question became, 1) Do we rate the occurrence and the detection of the failure mode, or 2) Do we rate the occurrence and the detection of the individual causes of the failure mode? (See Figure 2.1)

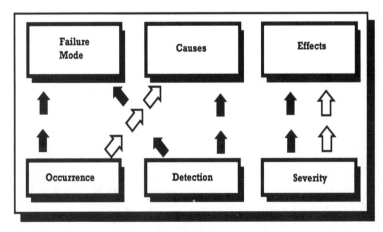

Figure 2.1

The team should decide and agree upon which approach to use. Either way you will get the same answers. Rating the occurrence and the detection of the causes is more direct and the most recent forms reflect this by locating each scale directly behind the column to which the rating applies. (See Figure 2.2) Examples of this are provided in the section on constructing FMEA.

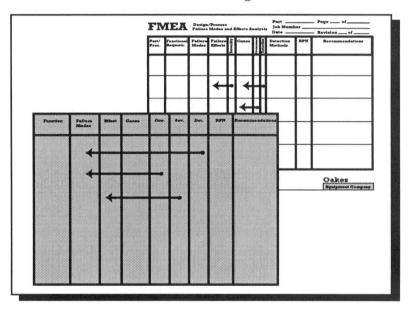

Figure 2.2

Regardless of the approach, the solutions for addressing the failure modes that have been selected via the FMEA analysis must be assessed through the causes listed in the FMEA.

Tailoring the rating scales and establishing very specific definitions for each of the numbers in the scales prior to actual FMEA development will save on development time and improve the accuracy of the ratings from each team member. As mentioned, a common practice for some organizations is to transfer existing scale guidelines or generic scales from company workbooks directly to the internal FMEA procedures. Many of these scales do not provide distinct definitions for each number. This may lead the team to unnecessarily debate the merit of two or three numbers that fall under the same definition! In addition, some of these generic scales from existing handbooks may not apply to the organization! Each scale must reflect:

Occurrence-	The historical quality of that organizations products
Severity-	The nature of the organization's products
Detection-	The operating policies and standard operating procedures of the organization.

The readers can compare their products, processes or services to other very different organizations and think of the subtle or drastic differences that will impact these scales. Example of these scales and suggestions on tailoring each them are provided in the section on constructing FMEA.

Ground Rule 4. Develop each column in the FMEA independently.

A major problem that all team members encounter is losing focus of the specific task being addressed in the FMEA. For example, it is not uncommon to begin with the task of listing the failure modes and quickly and frequently discussing some other column in the FMEA, what I call the "what if" syndrome. For example, the discussion begins by asking simply, How could the design fail? An answer to this question is immediately challenged by the question, What if the customer does not perceive this failure mode to be severe? This jump from the failure mode column to the severity column places the task of developing the failure mode column in the FMEA on hold while the team debates. Much later the team manages to get back on track, back to this failure mode and immediately someone raises the question, What if this failure mode can be easily detected? The team has now jumped from the failure mode column to the detection column. Someone loudly asks, What if this solution is implemented for fixing this failure mode? This causes the team to prematurely jump into the recommendations column. It is possible for the "what ifs" to remove the topic of FMEA completely out of the team discussion! A great deal of discussion has occurred without any real progress in the development of the FMEA.

A suggested ground rule for FMEA is that each column in the FMEA must be developed independently. Team members are not allowed to drift to another column while one column is under development. For example, when developing the failure modes column, answer the question, How could it fail? ... not, *if* it will fail. While, the latter question is relevant, it belongs in the occurrence column. Completely developing each column sequentially in the FMEA helps the team maintain focus and will increase the efficiency of developing FMEAs. This strategy should not be interpreted as suggesting that the preceding columns cannot be revised as new information is realized.

The FMEA team and team dynamics

Effective FMEAs require genuine teamwork. Even with the best intentions, teamwork can be discouraged. Therefore, a few words must be said on this subject. Some of the most common practices that lead to a breakdown in teamwork and suggestions on how to preserve teamwork are discussed on the following pages.

Who should participate in the FMEA, and how many people should be on the FMEA team?

A suggested, but not all encompassing, list of disciplines that must be represented in the FMEA are:

Research and Development	Materials Engineering
Design Engineering	Calibration Engineering
Reliability Engineering	Field Service
Process Engineering	Technicians
Quality Engineering	Production/ Manufacturing
Maintenance	Packaging

Two groups, Customers and Suppliers, have been intentionally omitted from this list to emphasis a point. In traditional practices, these two groups are commonly not represented in the development of FMEA, and many of the columns in the FMEA cannot be accurately developed without their input! More directly stated, in most cases, effective FMEAs cannot be done without input from the customer or the supplier. A frequent concern voiced by suppliers to the Original Equipment Manufacturers (OEM) or automotive companies is that suppliers are solicited for advice *after* a problem has occurred. Many of these supplier recognize substantial opportunities for quality and reliability improvement as a result of early input into the OEM's FMEA.

In defense of the OEMs, there may be proprietary information that cannot be disclosed. This is understandable on both sides; however, it is possible and in the best interest of the OEM and the suppliers to jointly develop specific parts of the FMEA where the final quality and reliability is dependent on their teamwork. Copyright agreements can be signed by the OEM and the supplier prior to the joint FMEA participation. (See Figure 2.3)

Figure 2.3

How many people should be on the FMEA team? A very large team will certainly supply more information; however, the cost to develop the FMEA, the time to complete the FMEA and the effort to manage this team will increase. On the other hand, a very small team will ensure minimum development cost and time, but the decisions made based on the information extracted from that FMEA will be of higher risk! The question now becomes, What is the minimum number of people that can fairly, without compromise, represent the interest of all the groups that exert influence on the final quality and reliability of this design, process or service? A rough guideline is 5-7 people.

Failure Modes and Effects Analysis

This number should make up the core FMEA team. This does not prohibit soliciting information for the FMEA from other individual not assigned to the FMEA team. Examples of how to efficiently manage and implement this strategy are provided in the section on FMEA Implementation Strategies.

Inviting the most knowledgeable individuals to participate on the FMEA team and later ignoring or dismissing any of their opinions that conflict with the team majority is certain to destroy the team dynamics. Some of the common practices, although unintentional, are represented in the following example.

A team of seven people has voted on the severity of an effect resulting from a failure mode using a scale of 1 through 10. The individuals ratings are:

9, 8, 1, 10, 10, 9, 9

What number should be assigned to the FMEA?

Let's look at the possibilities.

◊   One alternative is to ignore the 1 rating. This is sometimes done and later rationalize by suggesting that some members of the team should be granted weighted votes on certain issues.

◊   Another alternative that has been suggested on occasion is to throw out the lowest vote and the highest vote.

◊   Another option is to agree with the vote suggested by the highest paid team member.

◊   One final option is that the team should assign the highest number suggested from all the votes.

Implementing any one of these alternatives or options is certain to slowly destroy the team dynamics in addition to generating an ineffective FMEA.

There are two other options that can be implemented that will preserve team dynamics and ensure the integrity of the information in the FMEA:

1) Team consensus

2) Median rating with a contingency strategy for outliers and splits

A team consensus of all the experts will reflect the lowest risk number or the most accurate number; however, this option is likely to be very expensive and time consuming for even the smaller teams.

The median rating with a contingency strategy for outliers and splits provides the low-risk, cost-effective approach for assigning one of these numbers to the FMEA. This approach also preserves team dynamics. The following example, shown in Figure 2.4, demonstrates the use of this approach.

Failure Modes and Effects Analysis

All of the seven team members have submitted their severity ratings for the effects of failure modes A, B, C and D:

	Team Members						
	1	2	3	4	5	6	7
Effect of Failure Mode A	9	*	8	10	9	8	9
B	7	8	2	7	9	9	7
C	8	3	3	9	2	2	8
D	7	7	7	7	7	7	7

Team member #2 did not feel qualified to rate failure mode A; therefore elected to abstain for this vote.

The first step is rearranging the ratings in ascending order and placing them into a matrix.

Failure	Effect	Cause	Detection	1	2	3	4	5	6	7	Median
	A			8	–	8	9	9	9	10	9
	B			2	7	7	7	8	9	9	OUTLIER
	C			2	2	3	3	8	8	9	SPLIT
	D			7	7	7	7	7	7	7	7

Figure 2.4

48

As depicted in Figure 2.4, a severity median rating of 9 can be directly transferred to the FMEA for failure mode A, and a median rating of 7 for failure mode D. Failure mode B has an outlier; one of the team member may possess some knowledge or have a different understanding on this effect. The team allocated five minutes to this team member to explain the reasons supporting this outlier. In this case, the team was made aware of a recent design change to an attaching component that reduced the effects of the failure mode from a safety hazard to a customer annoyance. The team again voted on this effect and the resulting median rating of the severity number was 4.

For failure mode C, approximately half of the team rated the severity of the effect of the failure mode low and the other half viewed this effect as very severe. Time was allotted to discuss these effects in sufficient detail and the subsequent ratings again were split. The team agreed to and assigned one of the members the task of investigating an independent statistical study to objectively assess the severity of the effects for failure mode C.

The specifications

Some of the tasks required of the FMEA team member are to anticipate how the design could fail to perform its intended functions or meet the specified requirement, why it fails to do so, and what can be done about it. In order for the team to be able to perform these task effectively, the team members must possess a sound fundamental understanding of all the design requirements or specifications. One prerequisite to FMEA is defining all the requirements defined in the various specifications and ensuring all team members acquire a working level understanding of these specifications. There are four specifications that must be understood and satisfied:

◊   The Engineering Specifications

◊   The Reliability Specifications

◊   The Quality Specifications

◊   The Customer Specifications

The engineering specifications include functional, physical, dimensional and chemical requirements. The reliability specifications focus on the engineering requirements operating in various environments and for specified times. The quality specifications focus on the techniques used to design-in and monitor quality. The customer specifications reflect what the customers want and expect from the design.

All of the above specifications can have different requirements, and they all must be satisfied to achieve the quality or the reliability goals established by the organization. Prior to constructing FMEA, the respective disciplines for each specification must ensure that other team members acquire a sufficient understanding of these specifications. An overview of each specification should be presented during an FMEA planning meeting. This overview can be followed up with supporting data or one-on-one meetings.

Summary

Planning the development of the FMEA before actual construction and implementation of the form will ensure its effectiveness. Some of the planning considerations to be addressed range from, Who will be responsible for the FMEA? to Which approach should be used for the development and the assessment of the FMEA?

The responsibility for the FMEA should be assigned to one individual, not a team; however; the actual development of the FMEA must reflect the efforts of a team.

Remember, when selecting the approach for developing the FMEAs, top-down or bottom-up, you must consider the program schedule, the allocated budget and the availability of the team.

Two tasks should be completed prior to FMEA: identifying the requirements and selecting the preliminary concept. Techniques for accomplishing these two task are QFD and Concept Selection. Changes or revisions in the requirements or the concept will require a reassessment of existing FMEAs or may require new FMEAs.

Process FMEA can be developed simultaneously to, but during separate meetings from, the Design FMEA. Information extracted from each one is likely to influence the development of the other.

Some of the ground rules that should be established during the FMEA planning phase include: selecting an approach for rating the failure modes or the causes, tailoring the scales to reflect the organization and developing strategies for preserving team dynamics.

Failure Modes and Effects Analysis

The FMEA team must be able to fairly represent the interest of all groups that influence the final quality and reliability of the design, process or service. Two groups that *must be represented* are 1) the customer and 2) the supplier. A copyright agreement can be signed by all parties and attached to the FMEA to ensure joint participation in the FMEA.

A Rating and Ranking Matrix can be used to select one number, the median, that best represents the collective opinions of all the members on the FMEA team.

Finally, it is important to ensure that all FMEA team members must have or acquire a working level understanding of *all design requirements* or design specifications before they can be expected to contribute to the development of an effective FMEA. The four specifications that must be understood are:

◊   The Engineering Specifications

◊   The Reliability Specifications

◊   The Quality Specifications

◊   The Customer Specifications

Chapter Three:
Constructing the
FMEA

There are several formats or versions of the FMEA form. One objective of this book is to provide a comparison between them to assist the reader in selecting or designing a form that best fits a specific organization. Many of these forms are depicted in the appendix in the section on Industry Specific FMEA Forms. However, before making these comparisons, it is recommended that the reader review this section on constructing FMEA.

Each column in the FMEA, shown in Figure 3.1, has been assigned a number identifying eleven elements in this version of the form. Each of these elements will be presented in detail.

Element **#1** The FMEA *Heading* (Figure 3.2)

As mentioned, the FMEA is a diary and FMEAs should eventually be developed for all new and existing designs, processes and services. It is important to design the FMEA heading to capture all the necessary information to accurately identify:

a) What is this FMEA on?

b) Who is involved in the development of this FMEA?

c) What will be influenced by this FMEA?

d) When was this FMEA initiated?

e) What was the latest entry to this FMEA?

f) Who is maintaining the FMEA and approves revisions to the FMEA?

The example of this heading includes (Design/Process/Service), implying that this form can be used for any one of the three. The user simply has the option of crossing out the two categories that are not being used. When defining the category it is important to provide sufficient detail to distinguish the subject.

#1a

An example of **Description (Design/Process/Service)** subheading:

Description (Design/~~Process/Service~~)
High Capacity Hydraulic Pump
Part Number 3133478907
Customer Number BP4-05-88
Note: Project Number 17540

Additional information that may be necessary to identify the FMEA subject can be included under this subheading. The important thing to remember for this subheading is to use whatever system is in place within the organization to sufficiently identify and track the FMEA through the life of the design.

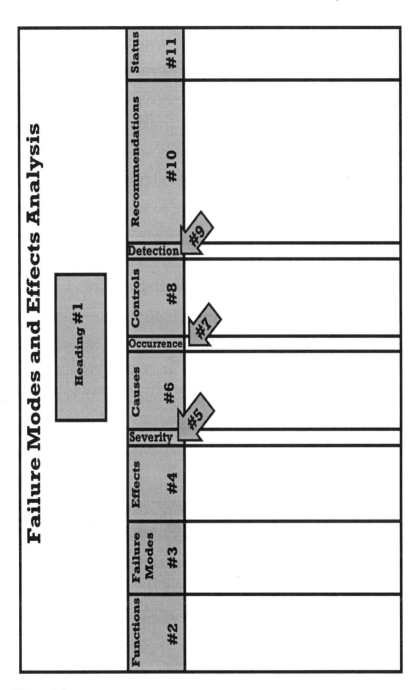

Figure 3.1

Failure Modes and Effects Analysis

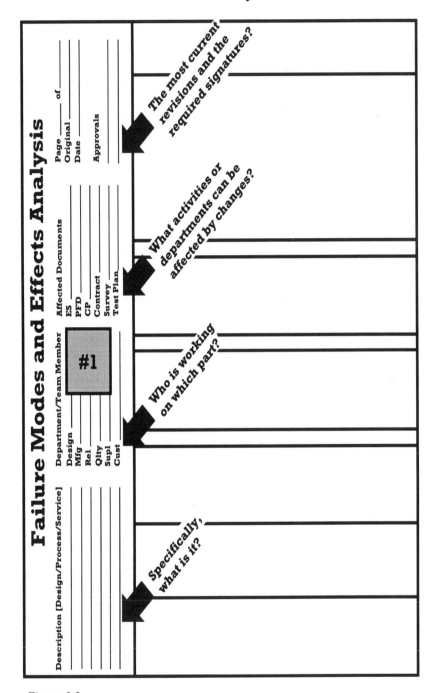

Figure 3.2

#1b

An example of the **Department/Team Member** sub-heading:

Department/Team Members
Design: Bill Ferlin (FMEA Responsibility)
Mfg.: Carl Garbe (Process & Packaging)
Rel.: Dave Herbert
Qlty.: Louis T. Horvath (Customer Liaison)
Supl.: Teleflex/Lincoln Brass/United Technology
Cust.: Detroit & Cleveland Assembly Plants

Identifying and listing the names of all the team members in the heading on the first page of the FMEA will provide the team members and all other subscribers to the FMEA with quick access for the development and the maintenance of the FMEA, as well as for future problem solving. The first column identifies the department or activity represented followed by the name of that individual. Additional information can be appended to the individuals name such as other groups the individual is representing or other special assignments for that individual. A translation of the example above shows that the engineering department is represented by Bill Ferlin; he also is responsible for the development and the maintenance of the FMEA. The manufacturing department is represented by Carl Garbe, who also represents the process and the packing concerns. Teleflex, Lincoln Brass and United Technology are supplying components to this design, and the customers have been identified as two assembly plants in Detroit and Cleveland.

#1C

An example of **Affected Documents** subheading:

The output of the FMEA is change! Hopefully, through effective FMEAs this will mean cost-effective changes resulting in improved quality and improved reliability. FMEA, similar to a diary, is dynamic, often subjected to changes throughout the life of the design, process or service. Many of these changes occur during the design's *saleable life* (not to be confused with the design life) will cause changes to other related activities within and outside of the organization.

Affected Documents

ES:	Engineering Specification 3135949842
PFD:	Ohio Plant Number 3 - Pump Assembly Line
CP:	Manufacturing Control Plan - B. Barth
Contract:	Quality Contract Lincoln Brass (PURCHASING-313)
Survey:	Preliminary Facility Survey (SQE - 1994)
Test Plan:	TBD

As shown in the previous example, the Engineering Specification (ES) has been identified. All changes, specifically the identification of "control characteristics," must be reflected in this specification. In addition, changes identified in the design and the process FMEAs that influence the process must be incorporated in the Process Flow Diagram (PFD). Some examples of changes to the preliminary PFD or existing PFD are revisions to the sequence of operations and inserting control points for checking the quality of a control characteristic identified in the FMEA.

All the information, critical to quality and reliability, extracted from the FMEA must be documented in a manufacturing plan and transferred to the process. This document is commonly referred to as a Control Plan (CP). The control plan is a detailed set of instructions that direct the day-to-day manufacturing operations. The control plan ensures that the designed-in quality and reliability is preserved during manufacturing, packaging and shipping and captured in the final products.

Over the last several years, some purchasing contracts have started specifying quality and reliability targets. This has become more prevalent during the past few years. Again, information extracted from the FMEA will provide insight for specifying these targets that are most likely to reflect the actual quality and reliability. For example, "Commitment Agreements" and "Quality Contracts" have been added to some of the more recent purchasing contracts. The Commitment Agreement may specify the use of FMEA, and the Quality Contract provides details such as the control characteristics and corresponding quality specifications. During the execution of the purchasing contract over the years, changes in the FMEA reflecting improvement in the design must be incorporated in the purchasing contract and, specifically, the quality contract.

The FMEA provides input to many other planning documents, activities and guidelines used by organizations. For example, the FMEA can be used to prepare and guide the supplier surveys. The FMEA can also provide information for developing test plans for cost-effective, efficient prototype testing.

#1d, e, f

The last block in the heading ensures that FMEA is maintained in chronological order, that the most current status is identify and the latest status has been verified and approved by the designated authority of organization.

Page: 88 of 120
Original: November 1, 1980
Date: May 19, 1994
Approvals: Peter Brown, Chief Engineer Supplier
             Mark Horvath, Design Engineer Customer

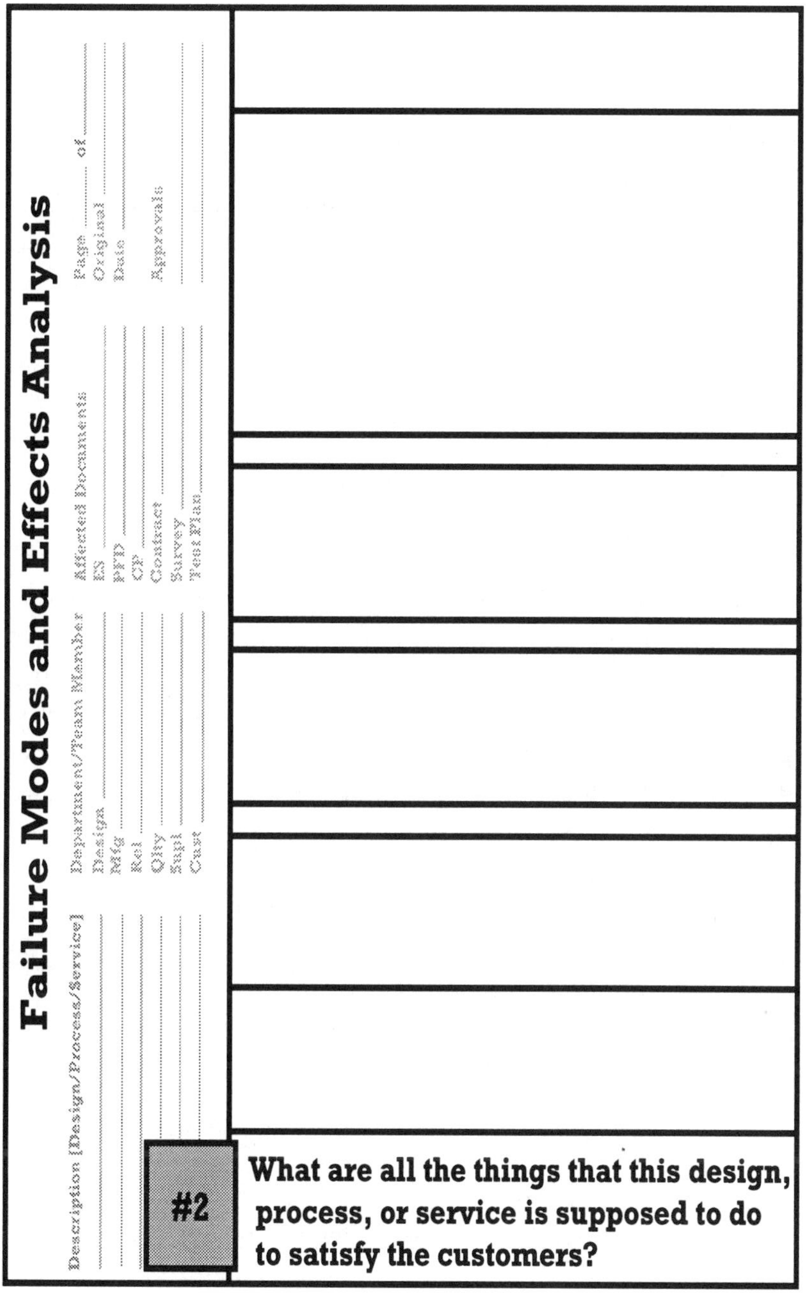

Failure Modes and Effects Analysis

Description [Design/Process/Service]

Department/Team Member
Design
Mfg
Rel
Qty
Sup
Cust

Affected Documents
EN
PPD
CP
Contract
Survey
Test Plan

Page _____ of _____
Original _____
Date _____

Approvals

#2

What are all the things that this design, process, or service is supposed to do to satisfy the customers?

Figure 3.3

Failure Modes and Effects Analysis

Element #2 The *Functions* (Preceding Figure 3.3)

What are all the things that this design, process or service is supposed to do to satisfy the customers? This question can also be restated as, What are all the functions?

Some of the common problems observed in practice when constructing this column in the FMEA are:

a) All function are not identified.

b) The description of the function is not concise.

c) The description is not exact.

d) The description is not in direct language.

In a effort to demonstrate these common problem, a disposable paper cup design will be used as the subject of this design FMEA (DFMEA). All the examples used are intentionally simple by design to ensure that the focus remains on the FMEA concepts and not diverted to the physics of the design. This has been thoroughly proven in the engineering community and in many of my seminars. Remember, this book is about FMEA not the example designs used to demonstrate the FMEA concepts.

#2a

When asked to define the functions of this cup, the most common response is, "It is supposed to hold hot coffee." Many of the teams proceed directly to the next column (failure modes) in the FMEA.

Functions	Failure Modes	Effects	Severity (1-10)
Hold coffee	?		

Failure to identify all the functions of the design is likely to result an incomplete list of the failure modes. Is there such a design that only provides one function?

I did suggest that one of the ground rules must be that the team is not allowed to talk about any other column in the FMEA other than the column that they are currently developing. This still holds true; however, when explaining how to do an effective FMEA, it may be necessary to break this rule. Experience has taught me never to violate these rules in the actual development of FMEA.

What are some of the other functions required from this design? In other words, what are some of the other things this design must do to satisfy the customer? The list below, while not exhaustive, is a sample of functions defined by seminar participants:

Functions

hold liquid	transfer liquid
insulate	stackable
look good	ability to be held in hand
crush resistant	disposable (environmental friendly)
contain liquid	resistant to spills when driving

Failure Modes and Effects Analysis

After developing the list of functions via a brainstorming session, the next logical step was to open up the list to a brief critique. Actually, this is the recommended two step approach for identifying and selecting ideas; however, in actual application the critique phase always manages to be incorporated in the first step. No team to date has been able to resist or delay the fun part or step two. Now questions were raised on some of the functions identified:

◊ **insulate**

◊ **disposable**

◊ **contain liquid**

◊ **resistant to spills when driving**

One of the team members pointed to two of the four common problems (listed on the previous page) encountered when defining the functions. The function **"insulate"** is not concise or exact, suggesting that this function should be broken down into two distinct functions as shown below:

General Function	Concise/Exact Functions
Insulate	1) Must keep the coffee hot
	2) Must keep your hand cool

An argument was made by another team member that the general function "Insulate" will suffice. The response to this is: the team should take care not to be too general because this may mask the resolution of the FMEA. For example, the concise/exact function defined to the right create two very different failure modes which produce two very different effects that each have different numbers for severity.

Functions	Failure Modes	Effects	Severity (1-10)
1) Must keep coffee hot	coffee is cold	taste bad	3
2) Must keep hand cool	burns hand	first degree burn	9

The different failure modes, different effects and subsequent severity ratings may not have surfaced by not breaking the general function **"Insulate"** into these two distinct functions.

This may not be recognized by defining the failure mode in general terms, and it is important to the effectiveness of the FMEA that the FMEA facilitator insist that all the functions listed are concise and exact. Taking the time to include all the sufficient detail is the key to working FMEAs.

Another point was raised: the function **"contain liquid"** is the same as the function **"hold liquid"** that is also listed. A lengthy debate among the team members ensued without any agreement in sight. When the team is in disagreement and sufficient resources (time) have been spent debating this one function, the team should include this function in the FMEA form. Everyone will agree that it is better to consider it and prevent it, should it indeed be a real issue, than to not include it and rely on the customer to identify it as an important function. On the other hand, the team must make a sincere effort to agree or ensure that the FMEA does not get bogged down with functions that are redundant or are not required by the design intent or the customers.

The function **"disposable"** was not identified by the FMEA team. This function was identified by soliciting the input from the environmental office of industrial operations. The team member from the quality office was assigned the responsibility of representing the interest of the environmental office.

The design engineer argued that the function **"resistant to spills when driving"** was not a consideration in this design. The marketing representative provided data that suggested an estimated forty percent of the customers expected this function. Should "resistant to driving spills" be identified as a function in the FMEA even though design engineering does not define this function as design intent?

When defining the functions for Failure Modes and Effects Analysis, the team must ask the question: How is this design used *and* misused *by the customers?*

Whether or not functions that are not design intent (but are expected by a large percentage of the customers) should be considered in the FMEA must be answered by the team. It is important to note that (although unfair) when some designs fail because of misuse, customers may perceive this as poor quality or poor reliability.

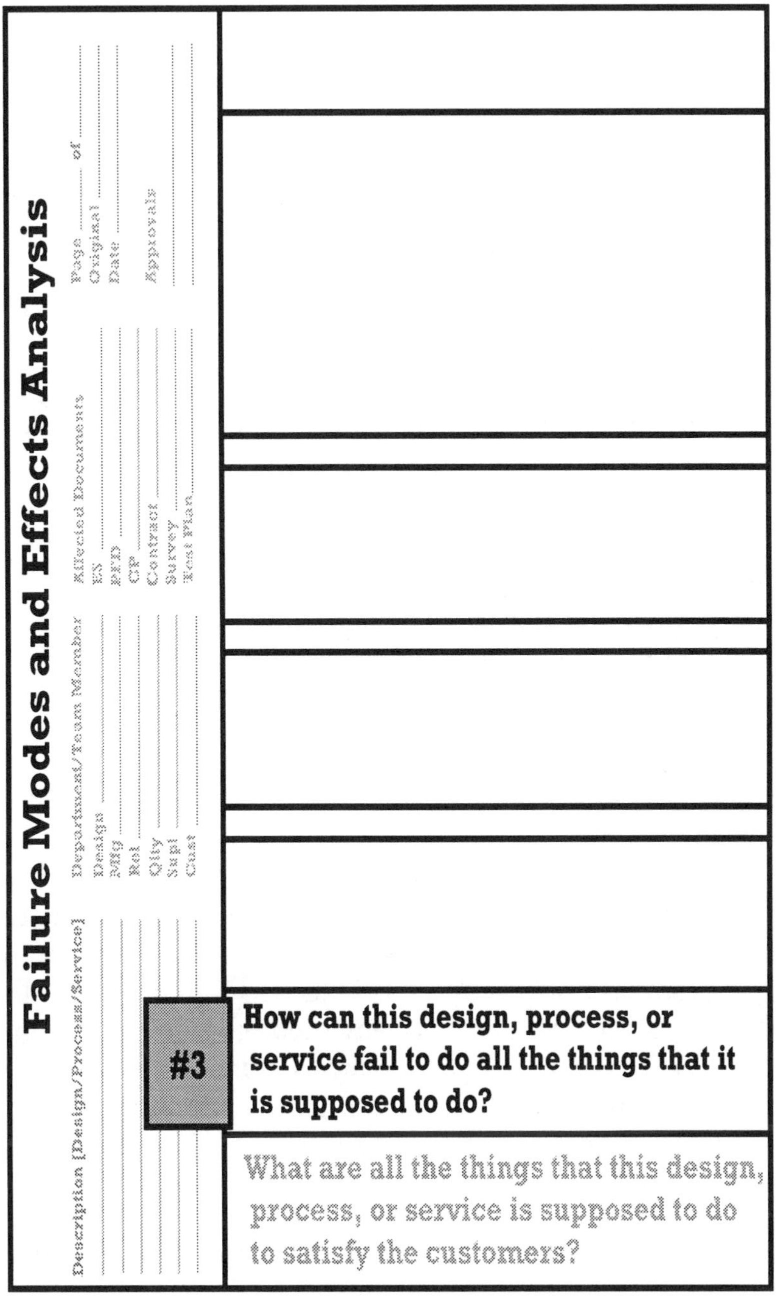

Failure Modes and Effects Analysis

Description [Design/Process/Service]

Department/Team Member
Design
Mfg
Rel
Qty
Supt
Cust

Affected Document
EN
PPAP
CP
Contract
Survey
Test Plan

Page _____ of _____
Original _____
Date _____

Approvals
_____
_____

#3

How can this design, process, or service fail to do all the things that it is supposed to do?

What are all the things that this design, process, or service is supposed to do to satisfy the customers?

Figure 3.4

Element #3 The *Failure Modes* (Preceding Figure 3.4)

When identifying failure modes, the functional approach (F) describes how the design, process or service could failed to preform the function defined in the previous column. Another approach to this is called the hardware approach (H). The hardware approach requires that each component or part is listed, requiring detailed design information. This information is typically not available or refined during the early stages of the design or the process development. In addition, describing the part defect does not necessarily identify how the design could fail to do what it is supposed to do. For example, the failure mode of the disposable coffee cup can be expressed using both approaches:

Functions	Failure Modes	Effects
Hold coffee	(H) Low paper density	?
	(H) Insufficient starch	?
	(F) Will not hold coffee	- mild burn
		- stains

As demonstrated, it is possible, using the hardware approach for identifying the potential failure modes, not to capture some of the effects experienced by the customers. In addition, since FMEA is implemented early in the design development stage when the team is working from a concept or the preliminary drawing, the functional approach becomes applicable for most new FMEAs. The following discussion will focus on identifying functional failure modes.

Often during the development of this column a failure mode will be suggested and immediately challenged by another team member who suggests that this failure mode is highly unlikely. The FMEA facilitator must remind the team that the likelihood of the failure mode will be answered in another column on the FMEA. The question to be answered in this column is:

Could this failure mode occur? .... Not, how often will it occur?

Recall two of the ground rules, identified in the overview section, that help the team stay on track and focused on the development of the FMEA effectively and efficiently:

a) Do not include every conceivable failure mode in the FMEA.

b) Confine the answer to only the question corresponding to the column in the FMEA currently being developed.

Using the paper cup example:

#3a

Functions	Failure Modes
Ability to be held in hand	**- Cannot be held by infants under the age of one year**

This example, an exaggeration of a conceivable failure mode, makes the point. Although the producers of disposable coffee cup cannot denied that this is a physical failure mode, it *would not* be transferred or documented in the FMEA for practical reasons. Failure modes that are conceivable but not practical should not clutter that column in the FMEA. Practicality and common sense must be exercised when using FMEA, as well as all other reliability, quality and statistical techniques.

#3b

Functions	Failure Modes	Effects	Causes	Occurrence
Stackable	**Will not fit inside each other**	- cannot pack - jam machine		1

The identification of first failure mode "will not fit inside each other" prompts comments from other team members that this failure mode happens very infrequently based on observations from the field or that if this occurs the machine can be easily be unjammed by reaching up and tapping the cup. The team has just jumped from answering the Failure Modes column question to answering the Occurrence column question and then the Effects column question. Again, jumping from column to column is a major contributor to inefficient and ineffective FMEAs. This practice can only lead to frustration for the team and excessive non-value-added time to the development of FMEA. FMEA is a step-by-step systematic approach. Each piece of the form is examined and thoroughly constructed before the complete most accurate picture of the future performance of this design can be painted.

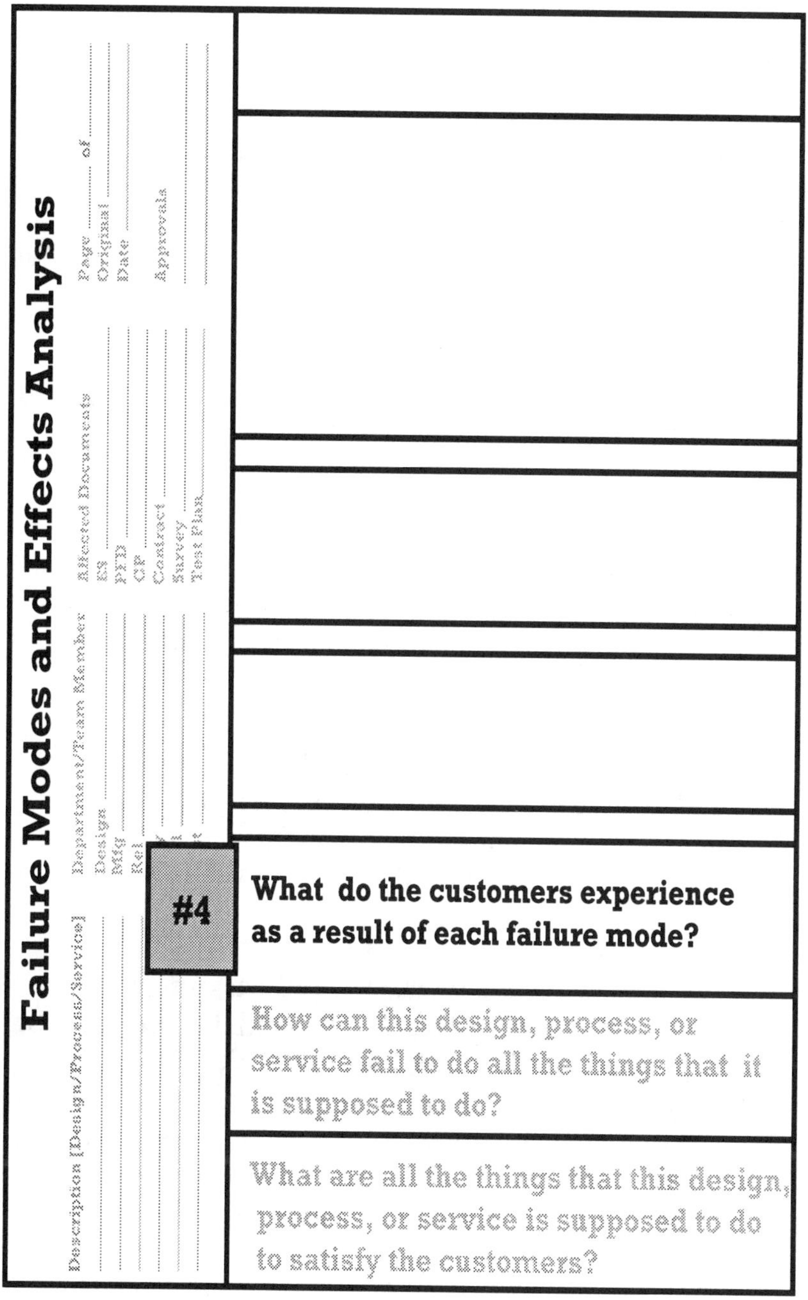

Failure Modes and Effects Analysis

Description (Design/Process/Service)

Department/Team Member
Design
Mfg
Rel

Affected Documents
ES
PD
CP
Contract
Survey
Test Plan

Page ____ of ____
Original ____
Date ____

Approvals

#4

What do the customers experience as a result of each failure mode?

How can this design, process, or service fail to do all the things that it is supposed to do?

What are all the things that this design, process, or service is supposed to do to satisfy the customers?

Figure 3.5

Failure Modes and Effects Analysis

Often the team may become trapped in a debate: Is the failure mode for the function described above a leak or is leak really the effect of the failure mode of the function or could it be that the leak is the cause of the failure to contain the coffee?

This can be very confusing and encourage plenty of unnecessary discussion.

Functions	Failure Modes	Effects	Causes
Must contain the coffee	**leak?**	**leak?**	**leak?**

Should the team experience difficulty trying to differentiate between a failure mode, an effect, or a cause, simply express the failure modes as the function in a negative sense.

Functions	Failure Modes	Effects	Causes
Must contain the coffee	~~leak?~~ **does not contain the coffee**	~~leak?~~	~~leak?~~

This approach does work. The only argument against this that has been presented to date is that it seems to be oversimplified and therefore cannot work. This thinking has been one of the major obstacles in the effective implementation of FMEA and all of the other reliability and quality tools. Often we loose sight of the problem or objective and all the effort becomes directed to the tool itself!

Keep it simple enough to get the answer, then stop. Plan and implement the more advanced, complex tools only if the answer is not achievable using the cheaper and timesaving tools.

Every individual within the organization has this obligation.

Element **#4** The *Effects* (Preceding Figure 3.5)

Describe the consequences of the failure mode. What do the customers experience should this potential failure mode occur? Three common practices that can mask the true consequences are:

a) Not from the customer's* perspective

b) Confusion between "local," "global," or "next higher" effects

c) Technical description does not capture the experience

*   The customers are defined as everyone who risk consequences of the potential failure modes regardless of whether they purchase the design.

#4a

The Effects column in the FMEA form is one of the columns that cannot be developed accurately without the voice of the customers. Often some effects are excluded from the FMEA and later this column is updated with early field data. This has been confirmed in many FMEAs.

Sometimes when you are too close to the problem you can't see it.

When developing the effects column, the team should actively solicit the customer's input. This information can come from marketing or field service and may exist in historical data banks, such as consumers product magazines, *Car and Driver* and government data and exchange programs, on similar designs:

◊   Marketing surveys

◊   Benchmarking studies

◊   Quality function studies

◊   Warranty reports

◊   Customer complaints reports

#4b

Some FMEA manuals make a distinction between different types of effects referring to categories such as local effects, global effects, next higher effects, etc. This is certainly a consideration when attempting to identify all the effects of a failure mode; unfortunately, asking the team to distinguish the failure modes by categories often adds more confusion and encourages lengthy debates. Simply ask the team and the customers: *What will you experience if this potential failure mode occurs?* Should the organization dictate that a distinction must be made between global and local effects, a helpful hint would be:

When developing the component FMEA the team should focus, but not exclusively, on the local/immediate effects of the component. When developing the system FMEA the team's focus should be primarily on the global/system effects.

For example, one supplier did not focus on local effects when submitting a component FMEA suggesting changes in the OEM's system design based on assumed system effects identified in the component FMEA. Some of these system effects were not physically possible because of the design configuration. The supplier was not given this information due to its proprietary status. The supplier was asked to redo that FMEA. The revised component FMEA served as input for the system FMEA, as well as provided better direction to the supplier for the improvement of the initial prototype components.

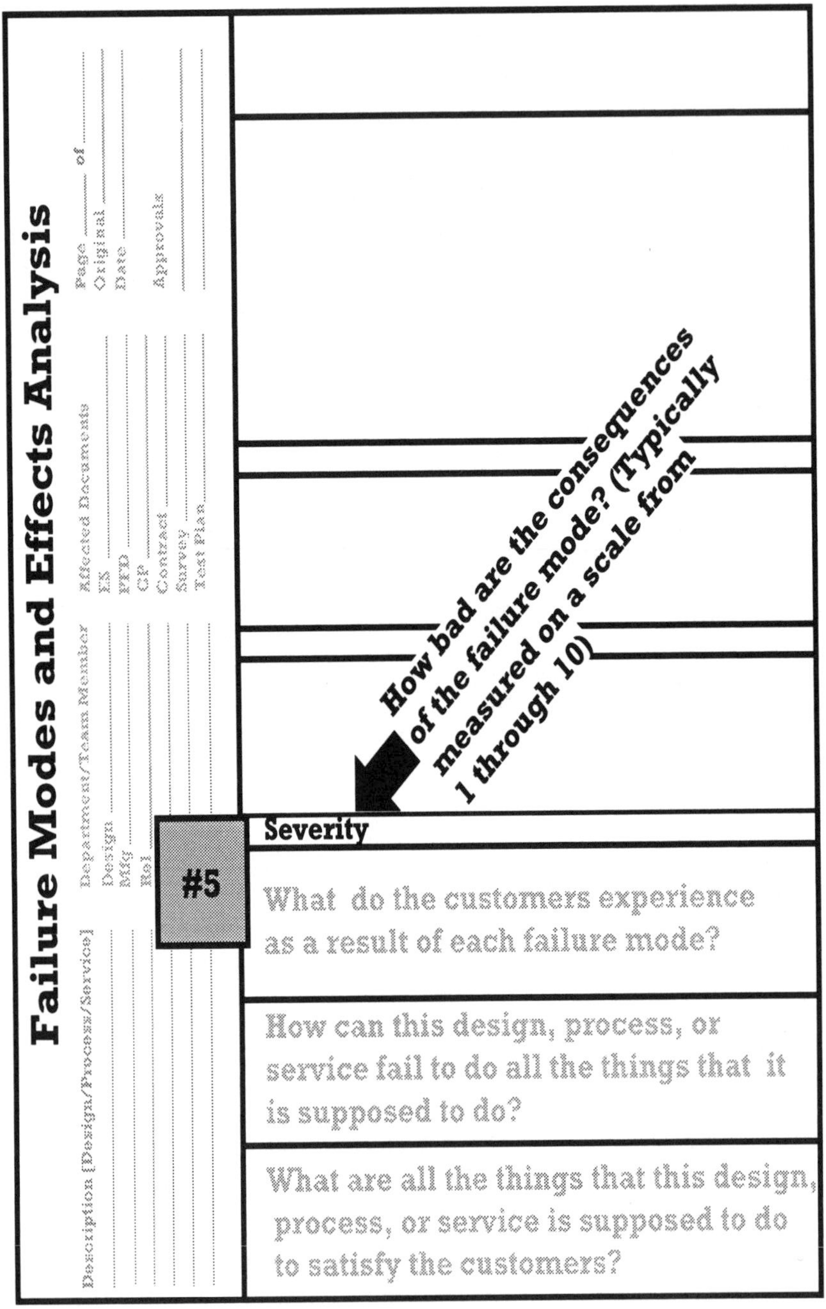

Failure Modes and Effects Analysis

Figure 3.6

#4c

Sometimes the technical description of the effect may not capture what the customers are really experiencing. If this happens the subsequent assessment of the seriousness of this effects can be underestimated. For example, an FMEA was conducted on a Surgical Sutures Needle Sub-system. The effect was initially written as "Excessive penetration force" with a subsequent severity rating of 4. When the effects were described in the customer's terms, the severity ratings were increased.

Functions	Failure Modes	Effects	Severity Rating (1-10)
Penetrate Tissue	- Low/poor penetration	(T) ~~Excessive penetration force~~	4
		(S) Increased Pain	7
		Bruises	6
		Scars	10

Whenever possible when describing the effects resulting from a failure mode, the description should reflect what the customers are experiencing via the senses. This will minimize the risk of underestimating the severity of the effect. In this example, two of the senses are 1) feeling and 2) sight.

Element #5 *Severity* (Preceding Figure 3.6)

How serious is the effect of the failure mode? This assessment of severity is typically measure on a scale from 1 through 10, the number 1 implying that the effect is not serious in the eyes of the customer or even that the effect may be unnoticeable by the customer. The number 10 reflects the worst possible consequences/effects resulting from the failure mode. A high severity number suggests:

◊ the safety of the customers is at risk.

◊ the failure cost will be extremely high as to jeopardize the financial welfare of the organization.

The definitions corresponding to the numbers in the Severity Scale depicted in Figure 3.7 are examples that may or may not apply to the reader's organizations. The definitions in this scale should reflect the nature of the products that are designed and produced by the organizations. It is suggested that these examples serve as a guide for developing a Severity Scale specific to the organization.

Severity Scale Description	Rating
The effect is not noticeable by the customer.	1
Very slight effect, noticeable by the customer; however, does not annoy or inconvenience the customer.	2
Slight effect that causes customer annoyance; however, does not prompt customer to seek service.	3
Slight effect that causes customer annoyance, prompting customer to seek service.	4
Minor effect that causes customer inconvenience; however, does not prompt customer to seek service.	5
Minor effect that causes customer inconvenience, prompting customer to seek service.	6
Moderate effect that causes degradation in the the design performance leading to a hard failure or a failure that will eventually cease design functions.	7
Significant effect resulting in hard failure; however, does not put the customer's saftey at risk and does not result in a significant failure cost.	8
Critical customer dissatisfaction effect, cease design functions, significant failure cost and slight safety risk (non-life threatening or permanently disabling) for the customers.	9
Hazardous, life threatening, or permanently disabling, or other significant failure cost that places the organization's ability to continue to operate at risk.	10

Figure 3.7

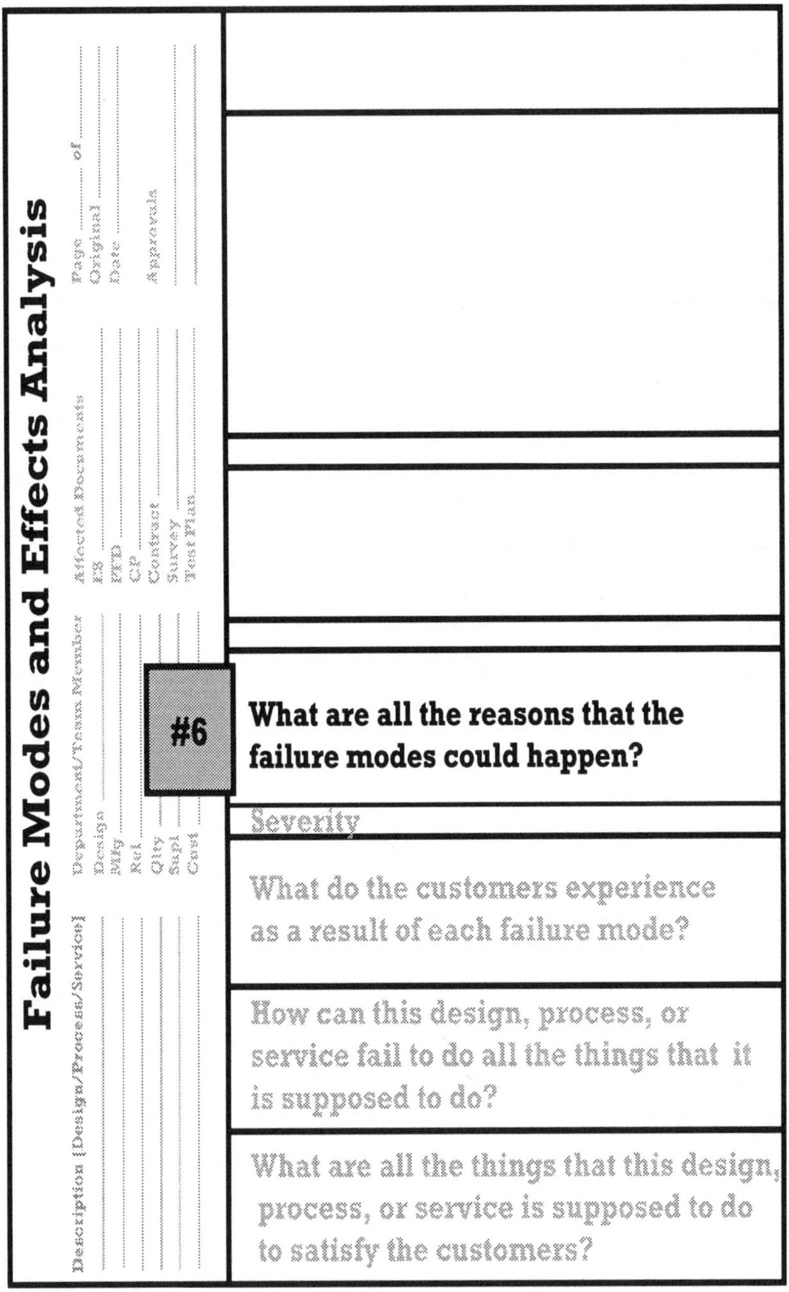

Failure Modes and Effects Analysis

Failure Modes and Effects Analysis

Description (Design/Process/Service)

Department/Team Member
Design
Mfg
Rel
Qty
Supl
Cost

Affected Documents
FS
FTD
CP
Contract
Survey
Test Plan

Page ____ of ____
Original
Date
Approvals

#6

What are all the reasons that the failure modes could happen?

Severity

What do the customers experience as a result of each failure mode?

How can this design, process, or service fail to do all the things that it is supposed to do?

What are all the things that this design, process, or service is supposed to do to satisfy the customers?

Figure 3.8

The preceding example of the Severity Scale shows that the magnitude of the numbers increases as the seriousness of the effect increases. Note that the number 9 is highlighted. Some organizations that have developed internal FMEA procedures require that special consideration be given to the potential failure modes that may produce effects that have estimated severity numbers of nine or greater.

For example, one procedure requires that all failure modes with severity numbers of 9 or greater, which cannot be reduced due to limiting technology or are cost prohibitive, must be transferred to and receive special consideration in the:

◊ Test Plan

◊ Manufacturing Control Plan

◊ Design Print

◊ Quality Contract in the Purchase Agreement

The above example is depicted in Figure 3.9. Once the team has identified a failure mode with a severity of 9 or greater they first investigate any recommendations that could reduced the number (Strategies for reducing these numbers are presented in the section on FMEA Interpretation.) If this number cannot be reduced, the team defers this to the Test Plan. A test plan is developed to assess this high severity failure mode and the outcome of the test either confirms or changes the severity status of the failure mode. If new information from the test provides insight for reducing the severity number below 9, the corresponding failure mode is removed from the special consideration status. On the other hand if the test confirms the original conclusions from the FMEA, the failure mode is transferred to the Manufacturing Control Plan, highlighted in the Design

Print and referenced in the Quality Contract appended to the Purchasing Agreement.

Element #6 The *Causes* (Preceding Figure 3.8)

For each potential failure mode list all the possible causes or reasons why this failure mode could happen. What conditions bring about this fail mode?

Some common mistakes made when identifying and writing causes in the FMEA are:

a) Some FMEA procedures restrict the search for causes

b) All causes are inserted into the FMEA form

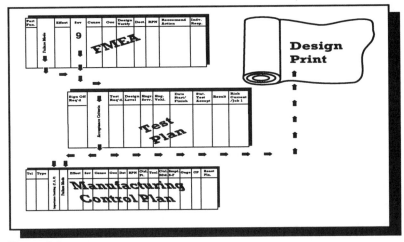

Figure 3.9

#6a

Some of the earlier FMEA procedures imply that when doing Design FMEA the identification and selection of causes attributing to the design failure mode should be restricted to design causes. This thinking can lead to inefficient solutions or prevent the actual solution altogether! Problem prevention or continuous improvement activities should be unrestrictive in identifying the opportunities for improvement. Look for and identify all the causes, regardless of the source, contributing to the failure mode. When developing Design FMEA, causes contributing to a failure mode can originate from:

◊   the Design.

◊   the Supplier.

◊   the Process.

◊   the Customer.

◊   the Environment.

◊   anyplace between the design and the customer.

One strategy for resolving or fixing a cause attributed to a failure modes is often applied without considering the overall cost or the scheduling:

~~Move the problem solving or problem prevention upstream~~

Upstream usually points to the design. What if it was possible to fix or prevent the problem more efficiently and cost-effectively by addressing a cause not in the design, but somewhere further downstream? This strategy is one of two strategies that must be considered for efficient and effective problem solving or problem prevention:

1)   The "Forgiving Downstream" principle

2)   The "Controlling Upstream" principle

Forgiving Downstream is accomplished by addressing process causes before implementing design changes or by tightening controls downstream of the process.

Controlling Upstream is accomplished by changing or upgrading the design or tightening the quality control of the incoming causes to the process. Typically, Controlling Upstream is more expensive.

Some examples of controlling upstream strategies commonly found in the FMEA Recommendations column are:

◊   recommending a material upgrade.

◊   tightening the tolerances.

#6b

The second most common mistake that is often made when developing the Cause column in the FMEA form is the practice of including all the causes in the FMEA that were identified in the brainstorming session.

*All causes do not contribute equally to
a potential failure mode.*

All the causes identified are likely to contribute to the failure mode that is being investigated; however, many of these causes may contribute very little to that failure mode. Only a few causes, referred to as "root causes," are likely to contribute to the majority of the failure mode. Using a Pareto chart (shown in Figure 3.10) the FMEA team can quantify and rank the contribution of each cause to a failure mode. As previously mentioned, it is not advisable to use the Pareto to quantify and rank the RPN.

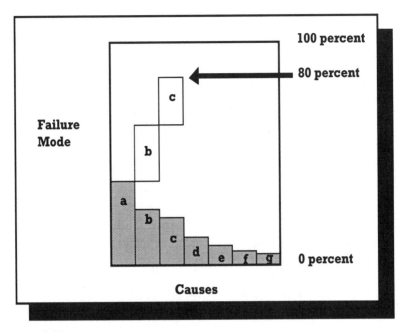

Figure 3.10

It is suggested that only the root causes are identified in the FMEA since the root causes a, b and c contribute to approximately eighty percent of the potential failure mode. An example, shown in Figure 3.10, depicts all the contributors (a through g) to the failure mode and only causes a, b and c as root causes for that failure mode. Should the potential failure mode warrant improvement based on the FMEA interpretation, allocating a fixed amount of resources toward resolving these root causes is likely to address approximately eighty percent of the potential failure mode. Allocating the same amount of fixed resources on trivial causes is likely to address less than twenty percent of the potential failure mode.

The following strategy is suggested for listing all the

suspected causes contributing to the failure mode and then extracting the root causes from the trivial causes to transfer to the FMEA form:

Step 1   Write down the failure mode.

Step 2   Review the appropriate block diagram (DFMEA) or the process flow diagram (PFMEA).

Step 3   Brainstorm all possible causes.

Step 4   Structure the brainstorming output using a Fishbone diagram (See Figure 3.11).

Step 5   Construct a fault tree if the Fishbone diagram appears to be incomplete

Step 6   Review the Fishbone diagram, screen out and circle the root causes (See Figure 3.11).

Step 7   Transfer the root causes to the FMEA form.

The objective *is not* to complete all seven steps! The objective is to identify all the potential causes and separate the few root causes from all the many trivial causes per the Pareto principle. The team should apply this strategy only when team discussion is not adequate to identify the root causes. When applying this strategy, the team should only execute the steps that are needed to identify the root causes. For example, if from sufficient warranty data or the engineering physics it is obvious that certain causes contribute significantly to a failure mode, the seven steps listed above may not be required.

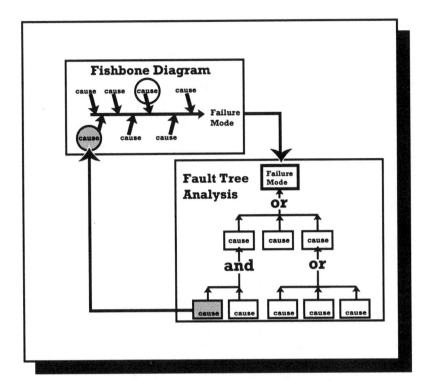

Figure 3.11

The team should try to screen out the root causes as suggested in step six. This step has a distinct strategy shown in Figure 3.12. The strategy depicted in the flow chart below begins with the fastest, lowest cost methods for screening out the root causes and proceeds to the more time consuming expensive methods.

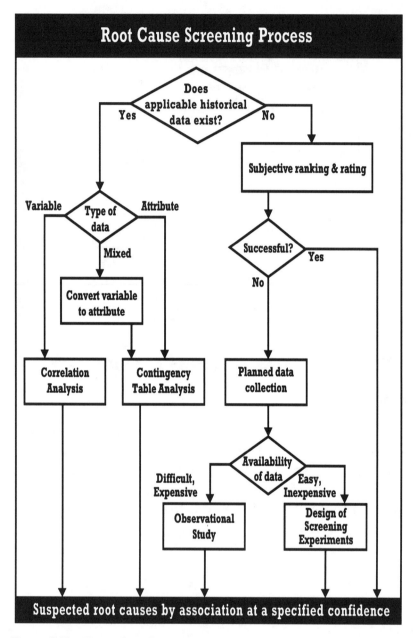

Figure 3.12 – "Logic for selecting/prioritization" from Hans J. Bajaria and Richard P. Copp, Statistical Problem Solving, 1991, Multiface Publishing Company, Garden City, Michigan

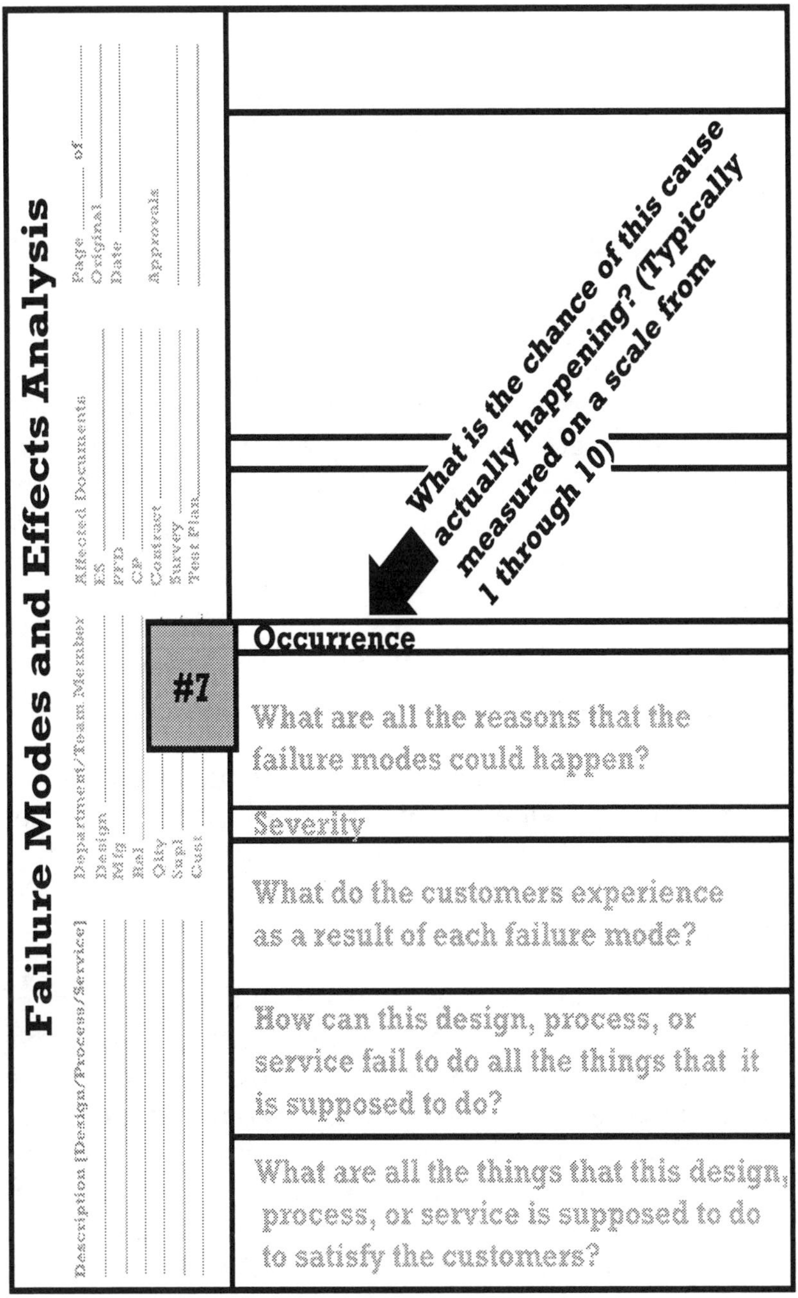

Failure Modes and Effects Analysis

Description [Design/Process/Service]

Department/Team Member

Design
Mfg
Rel
Qlty
Supl
Cust

Affected Documents

ES
PPD
CP
Contract
Survey
Test Plan

Page ____ of ____
Original ____
Date ____

Approvals ____

What is the chance of this cause actually happening? (Typically measured on a scale from 1 through 10)

#7

Occurrence

What are all the reasons that the failure modes could happen?

Severity

What do the customers experience as a result of each failure mode?

How can this design, process, or service fail to do all the things that it is supposed to do?

What are all the things that this design, process, or service is supposed to do to satisfy the customers?

Figure 3.13

Failure Modes and Effects Analysis

Examples of all the techniques shown in Figure 3.12 for identifying the root causes by measuring the strength of association between the cause and the failure mode are included in the appendix. The Subject "Quick" Index in the back of this book can quickly point out these examples.

Element #7 The *Occurrence* (Preceding Figure 3.13)

Recall early in the form, the "failure modes" question was asked: How could this design, process or service fail? Inevitably, when answering this question, someone always confuses this question with the question, How often will this failure mode occur? How often the failure mode or the cause will occur is answered in this column. Now there are two approaches that you can take when asking how often (occurrence):

1) How often will the failure mode occur?

2) How often will the cause of the failure mode occur?

Using the **first approach**, rating the occurrence of the failure mode, provides a more accurate estimated number of how often the failure mode occurs. The efforts for reducing this number will eventually lead to an assessment of the root causes.

Using the **second approach**, rating the occurrence of each root cause of that failure mode, may not always translate directly to the estimated occurrence of the failure mode. For example, last year's warranty data for a similarly designed air conditioning system, based on service calls, show that the failure mode "no cooling" is observed in approximately eighty percent of the service calls. Three causes a) damage O-ring at high pressure line, b) worn compressor seal and c) improper torque on connectors were identified as the major contributors or root causes to this failure mode. Historical field data and test reports show that the occurrence of each cause as:

a) Damage O-ring occurs approximately twenty-three percent of the time

b) A worn compressor seal occurs approximately thirty percent of the time

c) The fittings are improperly torqued about seven percent of the time

This subtle distinction between these two approaches must be understood by all team members. Once this is understood and an approach is agreed upon, the team can then rate the occurrence or select the rating number that corresponds with the definitions in the Occurrence Rating Scale. An example of the Occurrence Rating Scale is shown in Figure 3.14.

Occurrence Scale Description	Rating
Extremely remote, highly unlikely	1
Remote, unlikely	2
Slight chance of occurrence	3
Small number of occurrences	4
Occasional number of failures expected	5
Moderate occurrence	6
Frequent occurrence	7
High occurrence	8
Very high occurrence	9
Certain occurrence	10

Figure 3.14

This Occurrence Scale, shown in Figure 3.14, is too general and can act as deterrent toward developing effective and efficient FMEAs. Often the team may spend time debating the difference between an occurrence rating of 2 vs. 3 or 4. Team members are likely to have very different interpretations of general descriptions such as remote, slight and occasional. This can be partially remedied by assigning specific failure rates to each of the numbers in the Occurrence Scale as reflected in some of the more recent FMEA procedures. However, a problem still exists: the failure rates may not reflect the historical quality level of the organization or some of the divisions/plants within the organization.

Suggestions and examples on how to develop a very specific Occurrence Scale and on how to tailor it to fit the existing quality level are presented on the following pages.

For example, a company in the process of developing their internal FMEA procedures has researched its quality performance for the past two years. The manufacturing quality records, the field warranty reports and the engineering tests all suggest that the overall historical quality level of the company's products can range from 0.8 percent to 22 percent. This range was used to develop an Occurrence Scale specific to the organization using three steps:

Step 1)   The range was modified at the lower end of the scale from 0.8 percent to zero to accommodate any of the occurrences that can approach zero.

Failure Modes and Effects Analysis

Step 2) The range (0-25 percent) was divided into the first
nine numbers of the Occurrence Scale:

Percent	Number Rating
0.000 - 0.01	1
0.011 - 0.20	2
0.210 - 0.60	3
0.610 - 2.00	4
2.001 - 5.00	5
5.001 -10.00	6
10.001 -15.00	7
15.001 -20.00	8
20.001 -25.00	9

Step 3) The team acknowledged that when introducing a
new design, process or service or implementing a
change there is always the risk of occurrences
exceeding the historical quality limit of twenty-
two percent. Therefore; they agreed to reserve the
last number rating in the Occurrence Scale for this
possibility or when this risk may exist:

Greater Than 25.00   **10**

This information was used to develop the Occurrence
Scale shown in Figure 3.15. This scale was both specific and
reflects the quality of that organization saving development time and providing greater accuracy/truth in the
estimates. The percentages can also be converted into:

◊ Ratio

◊ Capability Indicators

For example:

Ratio: Many organizations use a denominator of one thousand or greater for the ratio when defining quality and reliability targets.

Organization	Quality/Reliability Target
Frigidaire	#/1000 Service Call Rate (SCR)
Ford	#/1000 Things Gone Right (TGR)
Johnson & Johnson	#/1,000,000 Defects per Million (DPM)

This ratio could be reflected in the Occurrence Scale of the FMEA. Some internal FMEA procedures have incorporated this into their procedures.

Capability Indicators are one of the quality performance measures commonly used by many manufacturing industries, specifically the automotive industry. The formulas for calculating these indicators vary, and, depending on which formula is used, it is possible to estimate the percentage of product out of specification or the estimated occurrence of the failure mode. Historical capability studies may be used to define the overall quality range, provided process stability has been demonstrated, for those industries routinely using capability studies to assess the quality performance. Examples of Capability Indicators are presented in the appendix.

Failure Modes and Effects Analysis

For example, calculating capability using a standard unit of variation (a standard deviation) based on a normal distribution:

Capability	Estimated	Ratio
8 Standard Deviations	0.00006	60 / 1,000,000
7 Standard Deviations	0.0004	400 / 1,000,000
6 Standard Deviations	0.0027	3 / 1000
5 Standard Deviations	0.0124	13 / 1000
4 Standard Deviations	0.0456	46 / 1000
3 Standard Deviations	0.1336	134 / 1000
2 Standard Deviations	0.317	317 / 1000
1 Standard Deviation	0.6172	618 / 1000

Other quality measurement criteria used by the organization can be used to define the Occurrence Scale for the internal FMEA. It is important to recognize when selecting and defining the Occurrence Scale that the organization tailor the scale to fit the organization's overall quality level and avoid ambiguity in the definitions corresponding to each number.

Occurrence Scale	Percent	Rating
Extremely remote, highly unlikely	Less than 0.01%	1
Remote, unlikely	0.011 – 0.20	2
Slight chance of occurrence	0.210 – 0.60	3
Small number of occurrences	0.610 – 2.00	4
Occasional number of failures expected	2.001 – 5.00	5
Moderate occurrence	5.001 – 10.00	6
Frequent occurrence	10.001 – 15.00	7
High occurrence	15.001 – 20.00	8
Very high occurrence	20.001 – 25.00	9
Certain occurrence	Greater than 25%	10

Figure 3.15

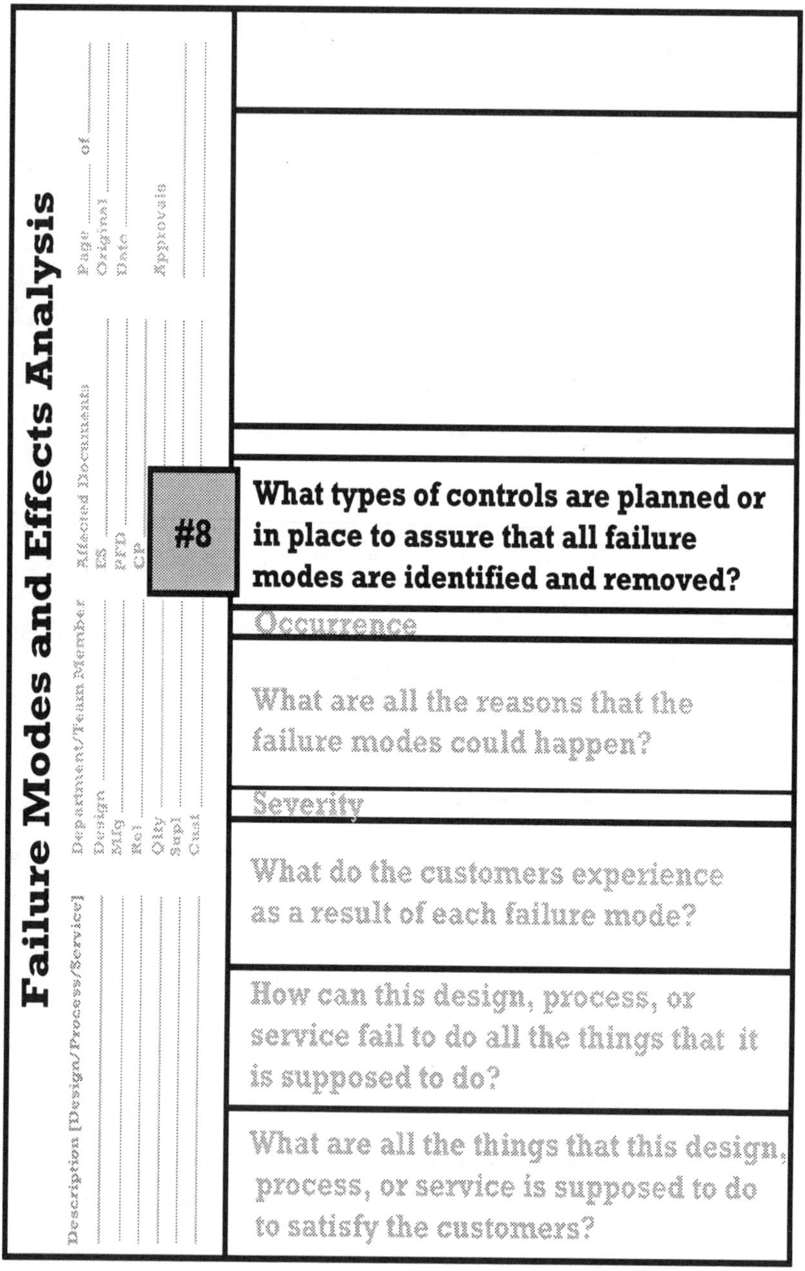

Failure Modes and Effects Analysis

Description [Design/Process/Service]

Department/Team Member
Design
Mfg
Rel
Qlty
Supl
Cust

Affected Documents
ES
FFD
CP

Page _____ of _____
Original _____
Date _____
Approvals

#8

What types of controls are planned or in place to assure that all failure modes are identified and removed?

Occurrence

What are all the reasons that the failure modes could happen?

Severity

What do the customers experience as a result of each failure mode?

How can this design, process, or service fail to do all the things that it is supposed to do?

What are all the things that this design, process, or service is supposed to do to satisfy the customers?

Figure 3.16

100

Element #8 The *Controls* (Preceding Figure 3.16)

In the following column of this FMEA form, Detection, the team will be asked to assess the effectiveness of detecting each failure mode or corresponding causes. Information on the type of controls/systems currently in place within the organization will assist the team in assessing the effectiveness of this detection.

Some example of the controls used for identifying potential failure modes and identifying the causes of these failure modes are:

Design Controls	Process/Service Controls
Design Reviews	Control Plans
Test Plans	Inspection Plans
Statistical Techniques	Audits
	Statistical Process Control

The primary objective of the FMEA is to anticipate the most important problems and try to prevent them from occurring or minimize the consequences of the problems once they have occurred. It may not always be possible to predict or foresee every potential problem; therefore, controls are often strategically placed in the design development process and the manufacturing process to catch any problems that were not anticipated by the team and prevent these problems from advancing to the subsequent phases and operations in the design development process or the manufacturing process. For example, the design review is commonly used as a control for the DFMEA. As the design evolves from the conceptual phase to the point where it is approved for manufacturing it may pass through as many as three categories of design reviews (controls):

Failure Modes and Effects Analysis

Type of Design Review	Objective	Specific Tools
Preliminary Concept Design Review (PCDR)	To evaluate & preliminary concept	• Quality Function Deployment (QFD) • (PUGH) Concept Selection
Detail Detail Design Review (DDDR)	To evaluate & approve the prototypes	• Statistical Comparisons • Design of Experiments • Statistical Tolerancing • Simulation Modeling
Final Production Design Review (PRDR)	To evaluate & approve the design for manufacturing	• Preliminary Capability Studies • Initial SPC • Initial Samples Submissions

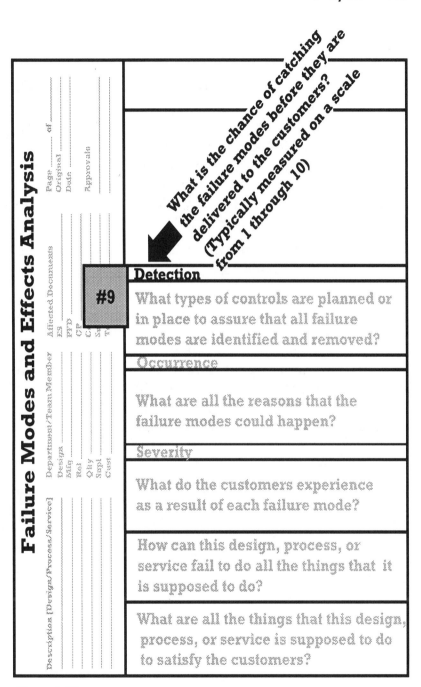

Figure 3.17

Element #9 The *Detection* (Preceding Figure 3.17)

What is the chance of catching this failure mode or the causes leading to this failure mode? Before detailed discussion on the detection and the rating scale begins, it is important to clarify what is meant by detection. Actually, there are two distinct definition of detection that apply to FMEA:

1) What is the chance of catching the problem before we give it to the customer?

2) What is the chance of the customer catching the problem before the problem results in a catastrophic failure?

This important distinction of how we define detection has not been recognized in many FMEA documents! It is important to recognize the difference. The **first** definition, What is the chance of catching the problem before we give it to the customer? is the question being asked in this column or element #9.

The customer is defined as any person or operation downstream from where the problem can be generated. For example:

Supplier	Customer	Deliverables
Final Customer	Marketing	• Wants & Needs List
Marketing	Design Engineering	• Requirements for the Design
Design Engineering	Test Facilities Process Engineering Manufacturing Supplier	• Test Plans • Design • Control Characteristics • Requirements
Process Engineering	Manufacturing	• Process Diagram
Supplier	Manufacturing Operators	• Materials • Components • Same as Above
First Operator	Operator Downstream Packaging Final Customer	• Product • Finished Product • Delivered Product

The **second** definition of detection applies to the Recommendations column in the FMEA form. Should the failure mode warrant recommended action and sufficient reduction cannot be accomplished in the occurrence and the severity, then consideration must be made to improve this type of detection: provide early warning (detection) for the customer that will allow the customer to take action to avoid a catastrophic failure. Some examples of this type of detection are:

◊   Warning Labels

◊   Built-in noise alerts to detect system deterioration

◊   Automatic system shut off switches, such as fuse protectors

Remember, improving the detection for the customer, although important, should be one of the last considerations. First, try to reduce the occurrence and the severity. Recall, the greatest opportunity for payback in quality and reliability for the customer, as well as the organization, is often realized in these first two considerations.

The Detection Rating Scale shown in Figure 3.18 is a example of scales found in internal FMEA procedures for some organizations. As illustrated, as the rating number increases the chance of catching the problem (failure mode or causes) are reduced. Some confusions can arise: "Does a higher number mean that the detection is better or does it mean that the detection is worse?"

A phrase that is easy to remember and that will eliminate the possibility of confusion as to what the numbers imply:

In FMEA ... big numbers are bad, and small numbers are good.

A very small number in the Detection Scale suggests that this failure mode or causes is almost certain to be detected before it reaches the customers or the next operation downstream from where the problem was created. The highest number on the scale shown, ten, suggest that the most likely way that the organization will become aware of this problem is when it receives complaints from customers. The higher the number, the higher the failure cost and the majority of this failure cost typically does not enter into the accounting system! What is the failure cost associated with each customer complaint in terms of customer perception or market share?

The Detection Scale shown in Figure 3.19 should, as in the other scales, be tailored to fit each organization.

Detection Scale	Rating
Almost certain to detect	1
Very high probability of detection	2
High probability of detection	3
Moderate chance of detection	4
Medium detection	5
Low detection	6
Slight detection	7
Very slight detection	8
Remote detection	9
Almost impossible to detect	10

Figure 3.18

Detection Scale	Rating
Very effective design review system, mature quality and reliability programs, state-of-the-art process controls	1
Effective design reviews, implementation of quality and reliability programs, highly automated process controls	2
Emphasis placed on design reviews, full quality program developed and implemented, currently training and partial implementation of reliability programs, automated process for the majority of operations	3
Quality program in place, awareness of reliability, no formal program, design reviews partially implemented, a mix of automated and human intervention procees controls	4
Quality programs developed but not fully implemented, no formal design review, some automated process controls, dependent on adherence to standard operating procedures	5
Initial stages of the quality program implemented, little automized process controls, partial implementation of operating procedures	6
Partial implementation of quality methods, sampling inspection plans and random audits, 100 percent inspection	7
Completely dependent on operator self-inspection with periodic quality control inspection, no implementation of quality methods, no formal procedures	8
Completely reactive to problems identified during manufacturing, no formal programs, some awareness of product quality	9
No system implemented, no awareness of quality, definition of product quality inconsistent – based on individual discretion	10

Figure 3.19

Failure Modes and Effects Analysis

This Detection Scale, shown in Figure 3.19, reflects the organization's controls, systems and the maturity level of its quality and reliability programs. The status of these controls must be assessed: Do they apply to each individual failure mode or cause? For example, within the organization it is possible for the existence of very advanced controls for detecting certain types of failure modes or causes. On the other hand, there may exist some very rudimentary controls for detecting other types of failure modes or causes within the same organization. In addition, some very basic criteria must be considered when establishing the Detection Rating Scale and when actually rating the detection for each failure mode or cause:

◊ If the failure mode/cause is inexpensive to check, assign a smaller number.

◊ If the failure mode/cause is obvious, assign a smaller number.

◊ If the failure mode/cause is easy to check, assign a smaller number.

◊ If the failure mode/cause is convenient to check, assign a smaller number.

It stands to reason that if the controls meet all the criteria listed above, the chance of catching this problem before it is shipped to the customer or advances to the next operation will be very good regardless of the state of controls for the organization. For this reason, it is important that the Detection Scale 1) reflect the organization's controls, systems and quality/reliability maturity level and 2) allow for the consideration of the four other criteria listed.

Element ~~RPN~~

Note: The Risk Priority Number (RPN) is intentionally deleted from this form. A complete explanation with examples of the RPN has been provided in the section on FMEA Interpretation. One of the primary objectives of this book is to restore FMEA as an effective tool. It is my opinion; I hope to convince you that we should break from the traditional interpretation of FMEA and replace the RPN with a proactive strategy for the interpretation of FMEA. A graphical technique for replacing the RPN is introduced in the following section on FMEA Interpretation. The RPN is the product of the three scales: the severity number multiplied by the occurrence number multiplied by the detection number.

Element #10 The *Recommendations* (Figure 3.20)

What are recommendations for 1) preventing the potential problems, 2) reducing the severity/consequences of the potential problems, 3) increasing the likelihood of detecting the potential problems before giving them to the customer and 4) providing early detection/warning for the customer for high severity potential problems?

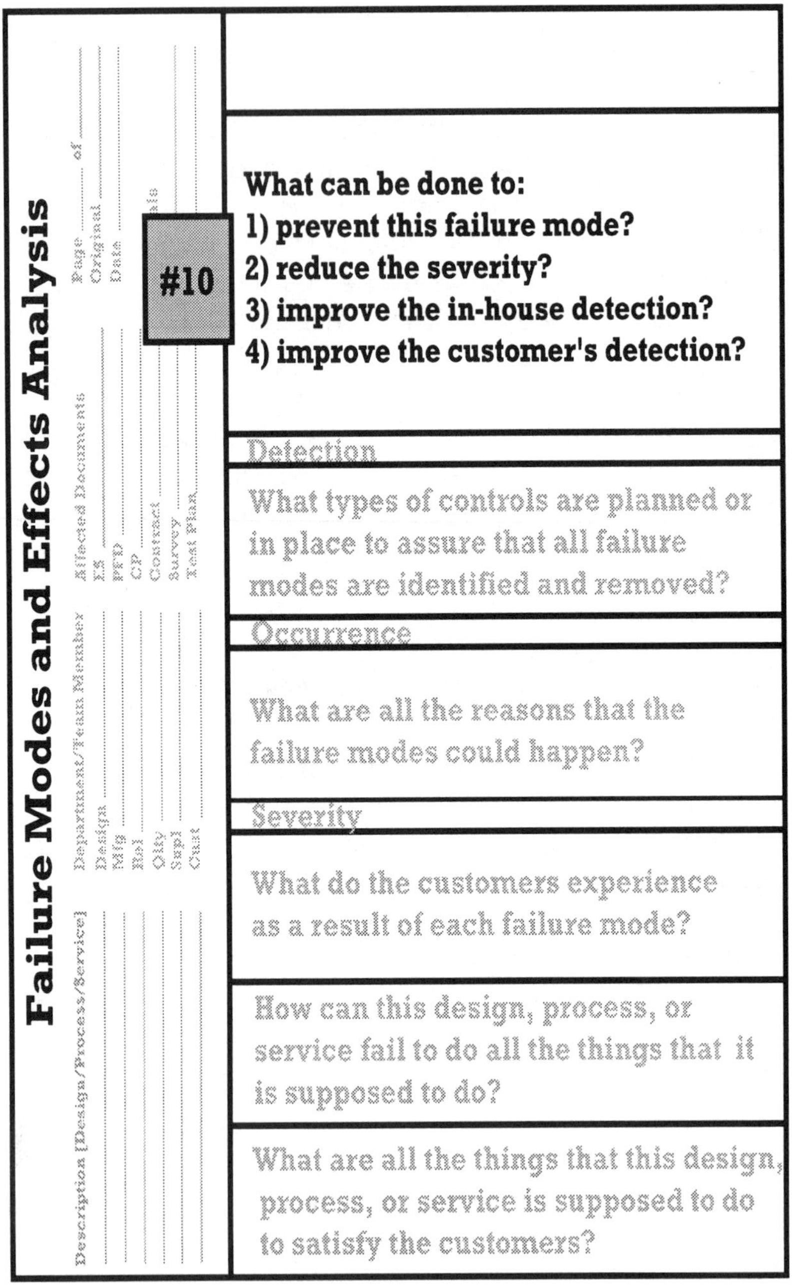

Failure Modes and Effects Analysis

#10

What can be done to:
1) prevent this failure mode?
2) reduce the severity?
3) improve the in-house detection?
4) improve the customer's detection?

Detection

What types of controls are planned or in place to assure that all failure modes are identified and removed?

Occurrence

What are all the reasons that the failure modes could happen?

Severity

What do the customers experience as a result of each failure mode?

How can this design, process, or service fail to do all the things that it is supposed to do?

What are all the things that this design, process, or service is supposed to do to satisfy the customers?

Page ____ of ____
Original ____
Date ____

Affected Documents
ES
PFD
CP
Contract
Survey
Test Plan

Department/Team Member
Design
Mfg
Rel
Qlty
Supl
Cust

Description (Design/Process/Service)

Figure 3.20

All FMEA procedures and manuals at the time of this writing suggest that, among other strategies for deciding on recommendations, the focus must be placed on the failure modes that result in the highest RPNs.

The RPN can mislead the team into addressing problems that are not as important to the customers and to the organization.

This has been acknowledged in some of the more recognized procedures on FMEA by supplementing the focus on the RPN with two additional qualifiers for deciding on the recommendations:

1) Assigning priority for investigating all failure modes that result in a severity rating of 9 or greater.

2) Failure modes that result in both a high severity and a high occurrence must also be given priority and special consideration when deciding on the recommendations.

Deciding and selecting the best recommendation to be implemented that will cost-effectively prevent the potential problems and minimize the consequences of the potential problems *is dependent on how the team reads or interprets the completed FMEA.* The next chapter is dedicated to reading or interpreting the FMEA.

Element #11 *Status* of recommendations (Figure 3.21)

Often, recommendations that have been made to address a potential problem identified in the FMEA are implemented with little assessment on the implementation cost and the resulting quality and reliability benefits anticipated from these recommendations. In addition, implementing recommendations with good intentions but without a thorough assessment may also introduce new failure modes or create interactions.

Organizations should not invest in any expenditures that will not eventually result in a quality or reliability payback for the customers, the organization and society.

Prior to approving any recommendations for addressing potential problems, the FMEA team leader should assign the task of thoroughly investigating the recommendation. The status of this investigation should be displayed in the FMEA form. This information serves three purposes. It :

1) ensures minimum risk for all recommendations that are implemented.

2) helps track individual assignments and coordinate the FMEA development within the overall development program.

3) provides documentation or references studies supporting or explaining high numbers in the FMEA that could not be or were not reduced.

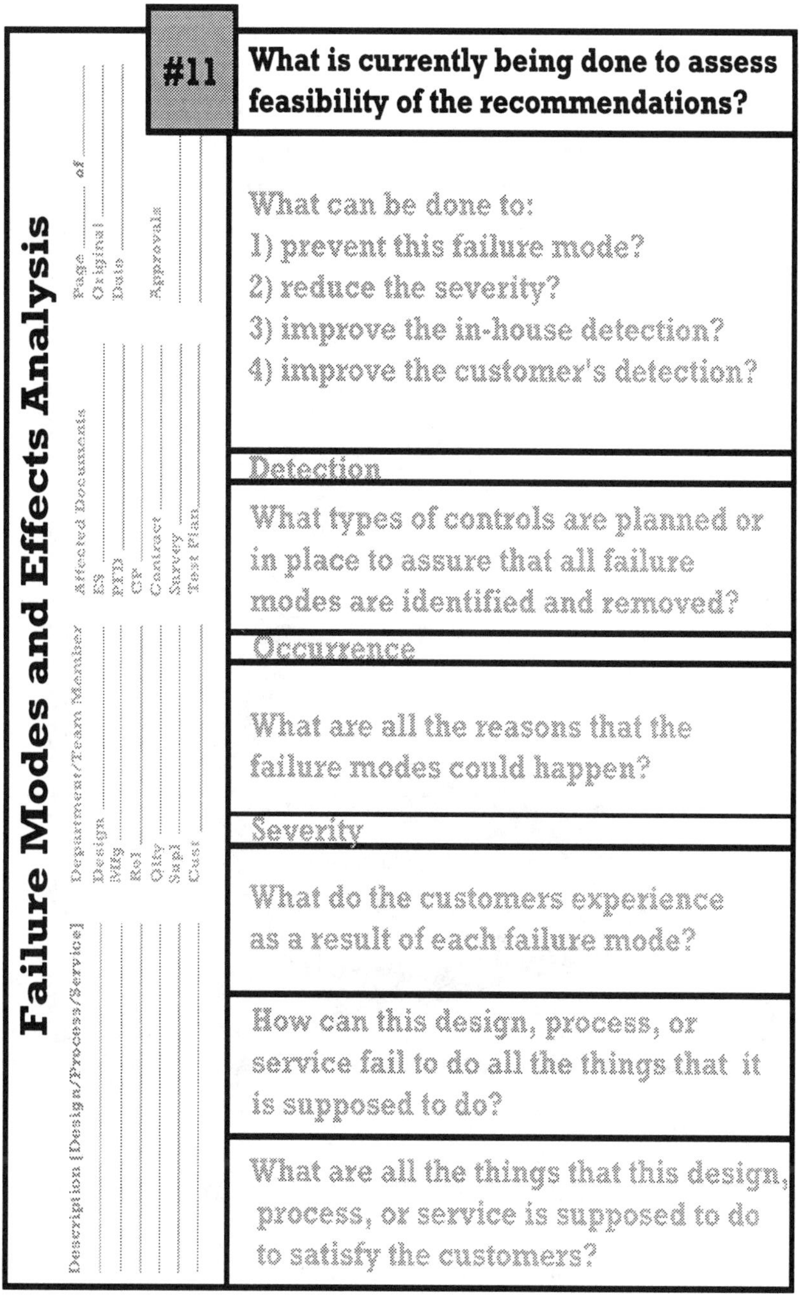

Failure Modes and Effects Analysis

Page ___ of ___
Original ___
Date ___

Approvals ___

Affected Documents
ES ___
PTD ___
CR ___
Contract ___
Survey ___
Test Plan ___

Department/Team Member
Design ___
Mfg ___
Rel ___
Qlty ___
Supl ___
Cust ___

Description [Design/Process/Service]

#11 — What is currently being done to assess feasibility of the recommendations?

What can be done to:
1) prevent this failure mode?
2) reduce the severity?
3) improve the in-house detection?
4) improve the customer's detection?

Detection

What types of controls are planned or in place to assure that all failure modes are identified and removed?

Occurrence

What are all the reasons that the failure modes could happen?

Severity

What do the customers experience as a result of each failure mode?

How can this design, process, or service fail to do all the things that it is supposed to do?

What are all the things that this design, process, or service is supposed to do to satisfy the customers?

Figure 3.21

The following example is a group exercise that can be used by internal FMEA instructors to demonstrate the preceding eleven elements/columns required to develop a complete FMEA application. The design for this example was selected for two reasons: 1) because of its availability in a seminar setting and 2) because of its familiarities to a wide audience.

The assignment is to apply FMEA to the overhead projector used during a seminar to identity the three most important recommendations that will cost-effectively improve the new overhead model currently being designed for next year. This assignment can be broken down into four activities:

1) Planning the FMEA

2) Constructing the FMEA

3) Interpreting/Reading the FMEA

4) Assessing and Implementing the FMEA recommendations

These results are from FMEA program exercises conducted at the University of Pittsburgh, Joseph M. Katz Graduate School of Business sponsored by Regina L. Lewis, Seminar Administrator for Professional Development and Executive Education and the University of Wisconsin sponsored by Roger Hirons, Director and Terry Lynch, assistant Director of the Center for Continuing Engineering Education.

1) Planning the FMEA:

Some of the planning tasks included selecting the team leader and agreeing on other team dynamics considerations presented in section two of the book. The team elected not to conduct top-down or bottom-up FMEAs. Due to time constraints and the simplicity of this design compared to other designs, the team agreed to develop a system FMEA. Also, because the team did not know all the individual component part numbers of the overhead projector, they elected to do a functional FMEA opposed to a part FMEA. That is, they would define the functions in terms of what the overhead projector is supposed to do to satisfy the customers. Finally, they agreed to rate the occurrence and the detection of the failure mode and not to rate the occurrence and the detection of each cause contributing to the failure mode.

The next task required before constructing or developing the FMEA form was for the team to understand and

Failure Modes and Effects Analysis

agree on the design. A functional block diagram, shown in Figure 3.22, was drawn for the overhead projector and reviewed by the team.

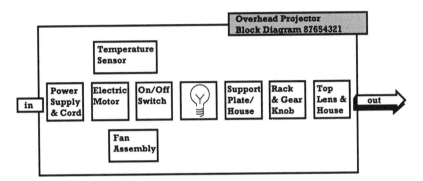

Figure 3.22

Constructing the FMEA:

#1 The **Heading** (See Figures 3.23 & 3.24)

The description, the team members and the original date were included; however, because this was an exercise, the remainder of the heading was left blank. In actual application it is important to include this information.

#2 The **Functions** (See Figures 3.23 & 3.24)

The team brainstormed a list all the functions:

- Supposed to light
- Should support transparencies
- Transportable
- Must locate image
- Project image
- Enlarge image
- Magnify
- Run quietly

- Should maintain operating temperature
- Run on 110/220 volts
- Adapt to two prong wall receptacles
- Focus image

- Insulate mat'l and user from heat
- Provide electricity
- Cool itself

These functions were recorded and later reviewed by the team. The team recognized some duplicate functions. They decided some other functions should not be transferred to the FMEA form and elected to rephrase others.

- Provide light
- Should support transparencies
- ~~Transportable~~
- Must locate image
- Should maintain operating temperature
- Run on 110/220 volts
- ~~Adapt to two prong wall receptacles~~
- Focus Image

- Project image
- Enlarge image
- ~~Magnify~~
- Run quietly
- Insulate mat'l and user from heat
- ~~Provide electricity~~
- ~~Cool itself~~

"Supposed to light" was rephrased to "Provide light." The functions "Transportable" and "Adapt to two prong wall receptacles" were deleted — transportable was not an issue for this design or any other designs in the companies history and, without a grounding third prong, the other function would be a violation of safety mandates. The other functions that were deleted were found to be duplicate functions.

Failure Modes and Effects Analysis

Description [Design/Process/Service]	Department/Team Member	Affected Documents	Page 1 of 2
Overhead Projector	Design: Brandon P.	Block Diagram: 87654321	Original: May 25, 1994
Model Number 3M-XML	Mfg: Lynn M. [packaging]	FTA: 7654321	
Reference Print 987654321	Rel: Lisanne P. [test planning]		
	Qty: Tom S. [customer liaison]		
	Supl: Z Castings, C Glass		

Provide light							
Support transparency							
Locate image							
Maintain safe operating temperature							
Run on 110/220 volts							

Figure 3.23

120

Failure Modes and Effects Analysis

Page 2 of 2
Original: May 25, 1994

Description [Design/Process/Service]

Overhead Projector
Model Number 3M-XML
Reference Print 987654321

Department/Team Member

Design: Brandon P.
Mfg: Lynn M. [packaging]
Rel: Lisanne P. [test planning]
Qlty: Tom S. [customer liaison]
Supl: Z Castings, C Glass

Affected Documents

Block Diagram: 87654321
FTA: 7654321

Focus image

Project image

Enlarge image

Run quietly

Insulate mat'l & user from heat

Figure 3.24

121

Failure Modes and Effects Analysis

#3 The **Failure Modes** (See Figures 3.25 & 3.26)

The team experienced some difficulty in two areas. Some of the original description of the failure modes were very general and confusion began arise as to whether the failure mode described was really a description of the effect or the cause. The table below shows the initial attempt at listing some of the failure modes.

Functions	Failure Modes	Effect	Cause
- Provide light	- Cannot see - Will not work	?	
- Maintain safe operating temperature	- Damaged wires	?	
- Focus image	- Out of focus	?	
- Project image	- Will not work		

The team elected to try expressing these failure modes as the "negative functions" in an effort to reducing the time spent discussion and to attempt to solve this confusion.

Functions	Failure Modes
- Provide light	- Does not provide light
- Maintain safe operating temperature	- Exceeds operating temperature
- Focus image	- Cannot focus image
- Project image	- Will not project image
- ~~Run on 110/220 volts~~	

The team did begin to experience some problem; for example, when the failure mode "cannot focus image" was identified, a few other team members suggested some "what ifs" that sidetracked the FMEA development: 1) they have never experienced this and 2) if this did happen, the user could, with the assistance of another person, physically move the unit to focus it. After some discussion, the team leader suggested that when developing the Failure Modes column, the team should not jump to the Occurrence column, the Recommendation column or any other column. The team reluctantly agreed and the FMEA was back on track toward developing the Failure Modes column.

The function "Run on 110/220 volts" was dropped from consideration by the team. As the team attempted to identify the failure mode for this function, they began to question if this function should continue to be evaluated in the FMEA. The argument was that the market for this design was confined to the United States and 110 volts was an industry standard and other power sources should not be considered. As the FMEA begins to develop, its resolution becomes clearer and unimportant issues begin to drop out.

Failure Modes and Effects Analysis

Description [Design/Process/Service] Overhead Projector Model Number 3M-XMH Reference Print 98765432 1	Department/Team Member Design: Brandon P. Mfg: Lynn M. (packaging) R&I: Lisanne F. (test planning) City: Tom S. (customer liaison) Supt: Z Castings, C Class	Affected Documents Block Diagram: 8765432 FTA: 763321	Page 1 of 2 Original: May 25, 1994		
Provide light	Does not provide light				
Support transparency	Transparency slides off glass plate				
Locate image	Will not locate image				
Maintain safe operating temperature	Exceeds operating temperature				
Run on 110/220 volts	Will not run on 110/220 volts				

Figure 3.25

124

Failure Modes and Effects Analysis

Description [Design/Process/Service]
Overhead Projector
Model Number 3M-XML
Reference Print 00Y05432.1

Department/Team Member
Design: Brandox R.
Mfg: Lynn M. [packaging]
Rel: Lisanne P. [test planning]
Qty: Tom S. [customer liaison]
Supl: Z Castinge, C Class

Affected Documents
Block Diagram: BY65432.1
FTA: 765432.1

Page 2 of 2
Original: May 20, 1994

Focus image	**Cannot focus image**
Project image	**Does not project image**
Enlarge image	**Will not enlarge image**
Run quietly	**Noisy**
Insulate mat'l & user from heat	**– Does not insulate mat'l** **– Does not insulate user**

Figure 3.26

125

Failure Modes and Effects Analysis

#4 The **Effects** of the failure modes (See Figures 3.27 & 3.28)

Once the team completed the failure modes, they moved on to listing all the effects or consequences for each failure mode. An example of the results of the initial attempt were:

Failure Modes	Effects
- Does not provide light	- Will not work
- Transparency slides off glass plate	- Undesirable for speaker
- Will not locate image	- Cannot use
- Exceed operating temperature	- Will not work

These preceding effects were too general or vague. The team quickly realized that all failure modes were either "undesirable" or would result in "will not work." They did not express what the customers would actually experience and would not provide and clear direction toward the objective of this exercise. Remember the objective of FMEA: to identify the single most important items to improve the design.

In this column, subtlety is the key to separating the important problems from the other problems.

If the team continues to identify the effects in these very general terms, than the recommendations are likely to suggest everything be fixed! It is commendable to say that everything must be fixed; however, this statement is often heard from people who are standing *very far* from the actual operations. A team should start by fixing the most important problems that are within its resources, and then, when this is done, they can tackle the problems that are identified as next important, and eventually, they may fix everything.

The team decided to identify the effects as the customers would experience these failure modes and try to look for the subtle differences between each failure mode. Accomplishing this would begin to separate the important problems from the other problems. The task of defining each failure mode as experienced by the customers was enhanced because an overhead projector was available for the team to manipulate or use during the analysis to simulate what would actually happen as a result of each failure mode. When doing FMEA, the team should have at their disposal last year's design or whichever design is most similar to the FMEA project. Some of the subtle effects were demonstrated by simulating the failure modes of the overhead projector:

Simulated Failure Modes	Effects Experienced
- Does not provide light	- Cannot see image
- Does not focus image	- Difficult to see image
- Will not enlarge	- Difficult for some people to see image

Without simulating these failure modes all the resulting effects were identified as "cannot see."

Failure Modes and Effects Analysis

	Department/Team Member	Affected Documents	
Description [Design Review Team]	Design: Brandon P.	Block Diagram: 8765432L	Page 1 of 2
Overhead Projector	Mfg: Lynn M. [packaging]	FTR: 765432L	Original: May 25, 1994
Model Number 3M-XR8L	Rel: Lisanne P. [test planning]		
Reference Print 96785432L	Qlty: Tom S. [customer liaison]		
	Supr: Z Casinga, C Glass		

Provide light	Does not provide light	**Cannot see image**
Support transparency	Transparency slides off glass plate	**– Speaker must hold transparency** **– Obstructs vision**
Locate image	Will not locate image	**Difficult to see partially obscured**
Maintain safe operating temperature	Exceeds operating temperature	**– Damage components** **– Burn speaker**
Run on 110/220 volts	Will not run or it cuts ...	

Figure 3.27

Failure Modes and Effects Analysis

Page 2 of 2
Original: May 25, 1994

Description [Design/Process/Service]

Overhead Projector
Model Number 3M-XML
Reference Print 987654321

Department/Team Member
Design: Nandor P.
Mfg: Lynn M. [packaging]
R&I: Insane P. [test planning]
Qty: Tom S. [customer liaison]
Sup: 2 Castings, C Glass

Affected Documents
Block Diagram: B7GG4321
FTA: 7654321

Function	Failure Mode	Effect
Focus image	Cannot focus image	**Difficult to see image**
Project image	Does not project image	**Cannot see image**
Enlarge image	Will not enlarge image	**Difficult for some people to see image**
Max quietly	Noisy	**Difficult to hear**
Insulate user & user from heat	– Does not insulate user – Does not insulate user	**– Damage components** **– Burn speaker**

Figure 3.28

129

As shown in Figure 3.31, one other function was dropped from future analysis and another function was added. As the FMEA progressed to the Effects column, it became more apparent that the function "Insulate the materials and the user from heat" was redundant to the function "Maintain safe operating temperature." However, during the process of examining the insulating function, one of the team members recognized the possibility of the projector not being grounded and emitting electrical shocks. This failure mode and the function "Insulating the user from electrical shock" were added to the FMEA.

#5 The **Severity** of the effects (See Figures 3.30 & 3.31)

The next task of the FMEA exercise was to prioritize the failure modes by rating the seriousness of the effects resulting from each failure mode. The team used the Severity Scale provided in this section, as well as asking themselves the question, As both a speaker using the projector and a student attending the lecture, what are the most undesirable experiences that they perceive from the potential failure modes?

The first step in rating the effects was to assign a scribe to record all the votes or ratings for each effects. The first rating prompted a question from one team member which was directly followed by a unrelated comment from another team member. After a short time, the scribe became confused as to what to write down and this task quickly deteriorated into chaos. The team leader suggested the team regroup and implement another strategy:

Step 1)   A paper is distributed to each team member, listing each failure modes and its effects.

Step 2)   Team members write down what they perceive as the severity number next to each effect on the paper.

Step 3)   The scribe collects all the papers and inputs the results into a Rating and Ranking Matrix (R&R) as shown in Figure 3.29.

Step 4)   The median severity rating, excluding outliers and splits, for each effect is transferred to the Severity column in the FMEA.

Step 5)   Fifteen minutes is allocated to discuss each outlier or split and the team is asked to revote on these effects.

Step 6)   Any of the outliers or splits that cannot be resolved are assigned to the appropriate team members for further study.

Rating & Ranking Matrix

Failure mode	Individual team ratings							Median Severity	Outlier
Cannot see image	8	10	8	9	8	8	8	8	
Speaker must hold transparency / Obstructs vision	5 / 4	7 / 4	6 / 5	5 / 4	5 / 4	5 / 6	6 / 7	5 / 4	
Difficult to see partially obscured	4	6	4	6	5	5	3	5	
Damage components / Burn operator	8 / 9	7 / 9	7 / 9	6 / 9	8 / 9	7 / 9	6 / 9	7 / 9	
Difficult to see image	6	5	5	4	4	5	6	5	
Cannot see image	7	8	8	9	9	9	9	9	
Difficult for some people to see	4	3	2	5	5	3	2	3	
Difficult to hear	7	7	8	8	8	7	7	7	
Electrical shock	8	9	8	8	9	1	9		Outlier

Figure 3.29

132

Failure Modes and Effects Analysis

Description [Design/Process/Service]
Overhead Projector
Model Number 38X-XML
Reference Print 93265432

Department/Team Member
Design: Brandon P.
Mfg: Lynn M. [packaging]
Rel: Lianne P. [test planning]
Qty: Tom S. [customer liaison]
Supt: Z Gaaiiags, C Glass

Affected Documents
Block Diagram: 8765432X
FTA: 265432X

Page 1 of 2
Original: May 25, 1994

Provide light	Does not provide light	Cannot see image	8
Support transparency	Transparency slides off glass plate	— Sender must hold transparency — Obstructs vision	5 / 4
Locate image	Will not locate image	Difficult to see partially obscured	5
Maintain safe operating temperature	Exceeds operating temperature	— Damage components — Burn speaker	7 / 9
	Will not turn on 110/220 volts spike	Run on 110/220 volts	

Figure 3.30

Failure Modes and Effects Analysis

Description [Design/Process/Service]   Department/Team Member   Affected Documents   Page 2 of 2
Overhead Projector   Design: Brandon P.   Block Diagram: 87654321   Original: May 23, 1994
Model Number 3M-XML   Mfg: Lynn M. [packaging]   FTA: 7654321
Reference Print 9876543321   Rel: Lianne P. [test planning]
    Qlty: Tom S. [customer liaison]
    Sup: Z Casings, C Class

Focus image	Cannot focus image	Difficult to see image	5
Project image	Does not project image	Cannot use image	9
Enlarge image	Will not enlarge image	Difficult for some people to see image	3
Run quietly	Noisy	Difficult to hear	7
Insulate user from shock	Does not insulate user from shock	Shocks user	?

Figure 3.31

#6 The **Causes** of the failure modes
(See Figures 3.32 & 3.33)

The team, using historical data (such as warranty reports, laboratory test, manufacturing inspection, rework analysis and past experience) from similar designs, began the task of identifying the root causes for the FMEA. For this exercise, they relied heavily on personal experience. They agreed to follow the seven step strategy for identifying the root causes proposed earlier in this section.

Failure Modes and Effects Analysis

Failure Modes and Effects Analysis

Description [Design/Process/Service]
Overhead Projector
Model Number 3M-XML
Reference Print 987654321

Department/Team Member
Design: Brandon P.
Mfg: Lynn M. [packaging]
Rel: Lisanne P. [test planning]
Qty: Tom S. [customer liaison]
Supl: Z Cumings, G Ginn

Affected Documents
Block Diagram 87654321
FTA, 7654321
Original: May 25, 1994

Provide light	Does not provide light	Cannot see image	8	– Msg. bulb – Burn bulb – Bad bulb
Support transparency	Transparency slides off glass plate	– Speaker must hold transparency – Obstructs vision	5	– Foot stop not adjustable
Locate image	Will not locate image	Difficult to see partially obstructed	6	– Top refelector hinge bent
Maintain safe operating temperature	Exceeds operating temperature	– Damage components – Burn speaker	3	– Fan motor defect – Temp. sensor defect
			9	

Figure 3.32

Failure Modes and Effects Analysis

Description [Design/Process/Service]

Overhead Projector
Model Number 3M-XML
Reference Print 98765432

Department/Team Member
Design: Brandon P.
Mfg: Lynn M. [packaging]
Ref: Lisanne F. [test planning]
Qty: Tom S. [customer liaison]
Sup]: Z Castings, C Glass

Affected Document
Block Diagram: 97654321
FTA: 7654321

Page 2 of 2
Original: May 25, 1991

Focus image	Cannot focus image	Difficult to see image	5	– Adjust knob threads dmg. – Lens Dmg.
Project image	Does not project image	Cannot see image	6	– Bad bulb – Bad switch – Bad motor
Enlarge image	Will not enlarge image	Difficult for some people to see image	3	– Bad lens – Bad knob assembly
Run quietly	Noisy	Difficult to hear	2	– Loose fan – Bad motor
Insulate user from shock	Does not insulate user from shock	Shocks user	?	No ground

Figure 3.33

#7 Occurrence of the failure modes (See Figures 3.34 & 3.35)

Once the team completed the task of listing all the root causes in the FMEA, they proceeded to the task of estimating the chance of the potential failure modes actually occurring. The team used the general Occurrence Scale in this section as a reference and agreed to follow the same strategy used to rate and rank the severity numbers earlier in this exercise.

Failure Modes and Effects Analysis

Description [Design/Process/Service]	Department/Team Member	Affected Documents	Page 1 of 2
Overhead Projector	Design: Brandon P.	Block Diagram: 8765432?	Original: May 28, 1994
Model Number GM-XML	Mfg: Lynn M. [packaging]	FTA, 765432?	
Reference Point 98765432?	Rel: Lisanne P. [reliability]		
	Qty: Tom S. [customer liaison]		
	Supl: Z Castings, C Glass		

Function	Potential Failure Mode	Potential Effects		Potential Causes	
Provide light	Does not provide light	Cannot see image	8	-- Mag. bulb / -- Burn bulb / -- Bad bulb	7
Support transparency	Transparency slides off glass plate	-- Speaker must hold transparency / -- Obstructs vision	6 / 4	-- Foot stop not adjustable	3
Locate image	Will not locate image	Difficult to see partially obscured	5	-- Top reflector hinge bent	1
Maintain safe operating temperature	Exceeds operating temperature	-- Damage components / -- Burn speakers	2 / 9	-- Fan motor defect / -- Temp. sensor defect	4
Power 110/220 volts	Will not run on 110/220 volts				

Figure 3.34

139

Failure Modes and Effects Analysis

Failure Modes and Effects Analysis

Description (Design/Process/Service)	Department/Team Member	Affected Documents	Page 2 of 2
Overhead Projector	Design: Brandon P.	Block Diagram: 8765432	Original: May 29, 1994
Model Number 3M-XML	Mfg: Lynn M. (packaging)	FTA: 7654321	
Reference Print 987G6432	Rel: Lisanne P. (test planning)		
	Qty: Tom S. (customer liaison)		
	Sup: Z Casings, C Glass		

Function	Failure Mode	Effects		Causes	
Focus image	Cannot focus image	Difficult to see image	6	— Adjust knob threads drug. — Lens Drig.	8
Project image	Does not project image	Cannot see image	4	— Bad bulb — Bad switch — Bad motor	9
Enlarge image	Will not enlarge image	Difficult for some people to see image	2	— Bad lens — Bad knob assembly	3
Run quietly	Noisy	Difficult to hear	9	— Loose fan — Bad motor	2
Insulate user from shock	— Does not insulate user from shock	Shocks user	2	— No ground	7

Figure 3.35

140

#8 The **Controls** for detection (See Figures 3.36 & 3.37)

The team was asked to improvise for this task. For obvious reasons this part of the FMEA could not be simulated in the seminar exercise. Instead the team elected to substitute the controls that identify each failure mode with the detection rating considerations listed earlier in this section:

◊ If the failure mode or cause is inexpensive to check, assign a smaller number: expensive **($)** vs. inexpensive **(-$)**.

◊ If the failure mode or cause is obvious, assign a smaller number: obvious **(O)** vs. not obvious **(-O)**.

◊ If the failure mode or cause is easy to check, assign a smaller number: easy **(E)** vs. not easy **(-E)**.

◊ If the failure mode or cause is convenient to check, assign a smaller number: **(C)** convenient vs. not convenient **(-C)**.

#9 The **Detection** of the failure modes
(See Figures 3.36 & 3.37)

The team then proceeded to rate the ability to detect each failure mode based on the their intuition with the assistance of the associated codes in the preceding Controls column. They also agreed to used the same strategy used for rating and ranking the severity numbers earlier in this exercise.

Failure Modes and Effects Analysis

Description [Design/Process/Service]	Department/Team Member	Affected Documents	Page 1 of 2
Overhead Projector Model Number 3M-XML Reference Print 98765432l	Design: Braxton P. Mfg: Lynn M. [packaging] R&D: Rosanne P. [test planning] Qty: Tom S. [customer liaison] Supl: Z Cusimqp, C Glass	Block Diagram: 97654321 FTM: 7654321	Original: May 23, 1984

Provide light	Does not provide light	Cannot see image	6	... Msg. bulb ... Burn bulb ... Bad bulb	?	-$/O/E/C	4
Support transparency	Transparency Slides off glass plate	... Speaker must hold transparency ... Obstructs vision	6	... Foot stop not adjustable	?	-$/O/E/C	3
Locate image	Will not locate image	Difficult to see partially obscured	5	... Top reflector hinge bent	?	-$/O/E/C	5
Maintain safe operating temperature	Exceeds operating temperature	... Damage components ... Burn speaker	9	... Fan motor defect ... Temp. sensor defect	?	$/-O/-E/-C	9
Runs on 110/220 volts	Will not run on 110/220 volts					

Figure 3.36

Failure Modes and Effects Analysis

Description [Design/Process/Service]
Overhead Projector
Model Number 3M-XMR
Reference Print BAY654321

Department/Team Member
Design: Brandon P.
Mfg: Lynn M. [packaging]
Rel: Roxanne P. [test planning]
Qty: Tom S. [customer liaison]
Sup: X.Castings, C Glass

Affected Documents
Block Diagram: 87654321
FTA, 7654321

Page 2 of 2
Original: May 25, 1994

Function							
Focus image	Cannot focus image	Difficult to see image	8	-- Adjust knob threads dang. -- lens Dang.	5	-$/O/E/-C	6
Project image	Does not project image	Cannot see image	8	-- Bad bulb -- Bad switch -- Bad motor	6	-$/O/E/C	4
Enlarge image	Will not enlarge image	Difficult for some people to see image	2	-- Bad lens -- Bad knob assembly	3	-$/O/E/-C	6
Run quietly	Noisy	Difficult to hear	8	-- Loose fan -- Bad motor	7	-$/O/E/C	2
Insulate user from shock	-- Does not insulate user from shock	Shocks user	7	-- No ground	2	-$/O/-E/-C	9

Figure 3.37

#10 The Recommendations
(See Figures 3.38 & 3.39)

The three most important failure modes identified in the FMEA were:

Failure Modes	Reason Selected
Does not provide light	High severity and Frequent occurrence
Exceeds operating temperature	High severity
Noisy	Moderate severity and Very high occurrence

It was also noted that the failure mode "Exceeds operating temperature" has a high detection number. This pointed out to the team that if sufficient reduction in the severity number is not achieved the team will recommend allocation resources toward improving the in-plant detection or customer detection. However, the team agreed that they should first concentrate on reducing the severity and the occurrence before investigating the alternatives for improving detection.

Should the team pursue improvement in the detection, the codes in the Controls column of the FMEA ($/-O/-E/-C) suggest areas where improvement can be made. Recall that:

$ implies that it is very expensive to check the failure mode.

-O implies that the failure mode *is not* obvious.

-E implies that it *is not* easy to check for this failure mode.

-C implies that it *is not* convenient to check for this failure mode.

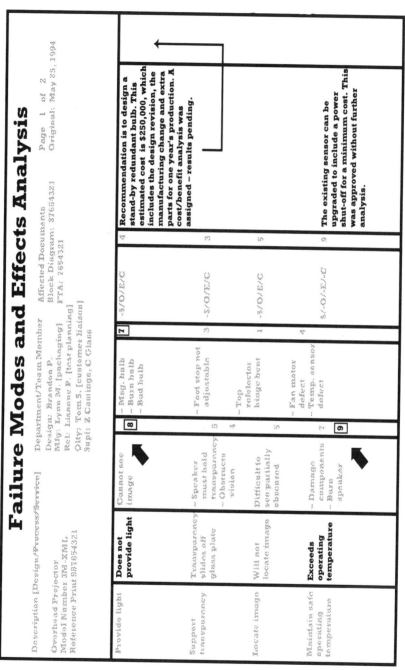

Figure 3.38

Failure Modes and Effects Analysis

Failure Modes and Effects Analysis

Description: Design/Product/Service
Overhead Projector
Model Number 3M-XML
Reference Print 987654321

Department/Team Member
Design: Brandon P.
Mfg: Lynn M. (packaging)
Rel: Jasmine P. (test planning)
Qlty: Tom S. (customer liaison)
Supl: Z Cushings, C Glass

Function	Failure Mode	Effect		Cause				
Focus image	Cannot focus image	Difficult to see image	5	-Adjust knob threads drag. -Lens Drag.	6	-$/O/K/-C	6	
Project image	Does not project image	Cannot see image	6	-Bad bulb -Bad switch -Bad motor	4	-$/O/K/C	4	
Enlarge image	Will not enlarge image	Difficult for some people to see image	3	-Bad lens -Bad knob assembly	2	-$/O/K/C	6	
Run quietly	Noisy	Difficult to hear	7	-Loose fan -Bad motor	9	-$/O/K/C	2	Recommend study to investigate the amount of noise attributed to motor and fan fastener system
Insulate user from shock	-Does not insulate user from shock	Shocks user	?	No ground	2	-$/O/-E/C	6	

Figure 3.39

#11 The **Status** (See Figures 3.40 & 3.41)

In reviewing some of the existing FMEAs it would not be uncommon to see recommendations that have been implemented where results produced little or no improvement to the failure mode! In addition, the cost to implement some of these recommendations may far exceed the benefits to the customer and the organization.

All recommendations that require significant resources or involve high-risk should be investigated and the results of these studies reviewed by the FMEA team. In the example, one of the failure modes, "Exceeding the operating temperature," did not require significant resources or involved high risk, and the team decided that it could be implemented without future analysis. The status for this recommendation was listed as "approved." The other two recommendations would require additional analysis and the status for these two was listed as "pending." These two failure modes would typically be assigned to one of the team members along with a scheduled completion date. This example will demonstrate one possible cost/benefit study for the failure mode "Does not provide light." The recommendation was to design-in a stand-by redundant bulb. The engineer felt that stand-by redundance would reduce the number of times that the user would not be able complete a presentation because of this failure mode.

Failure Modes and Effects Analysis

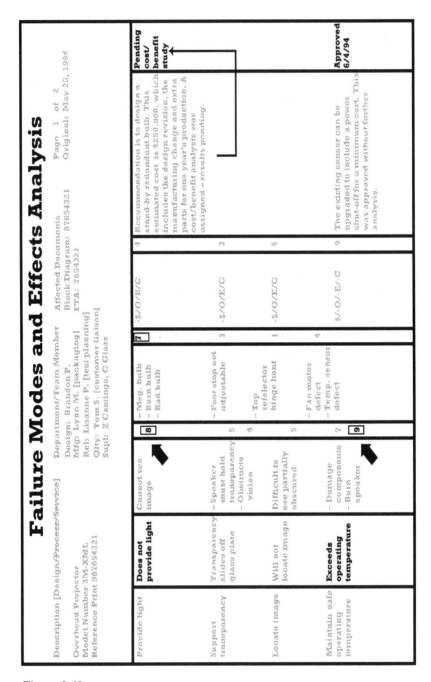

Figure 3.40

Failure Modes and Effects Analysis

Description [Design/Process/Service]

Overhead Projector
Model Number 3M-XML
Reference Print 3BY654321

Department/Team Member
Design: Brandus P.
Mfg: Lynn M. [packaging]
Rel: Lisanne P. [test planning]
Qty: Tom S. [customer liaison]
Supl: Z Castings, C Glass

Affected Documents
Block Diagram: BY854321
FTA: 7654321

Page 2 of 2
Original: May 25, 1994

Focus image	Cannot focus image	Difficult to see image	8	... Adjust knob threads drug. ... Lens Drng.	8	-$/O/E/-C	8	
Project image	Does not project image	Cannot see image	9	... Bad bulb ... Bad switch ... Bad motor	4	-$/O/E/C	4	
Enlarge image	Will not enlarge image	Difficult for some people to see image	3	... Bad lens ... Bad knob assembly	2	-$/O/E/-C	6	
Run quietly	**Noisy**	Difficult to hear	7	... Loose fan ... Bad motor	9	-$/O/E/C	3	Recommend study to investigate the amount of noise attributed to motor and fan fastener system
Insulate user from shock	... Does not insulate user from shock	Shocks user	7	No ground	2	-$/O/-E/-C	9	

Pending feasibility and cost/benefit study from Carl Garbe due 7/22/94

Figure 3.41

Failure Modes and Effects Analysis

For this example a cost/benefit study for the recommendation of a redundant bulb was investigated using the following steps:

Step 1 Review the block diagram and construct a fault tree of the current design, shown in Figure 3.42, to depict all the events leading to the failure modes.

Step 2 Estimate the failure rate of not providing light for the current design using fault tree analysis (FTA).

Step 3 Estimate the annual service cost for the current design (Failure Rate x Annual Production x Service Cost Per Unit).

Step 4 Calculate the total cost of the study, from engineering change to the estimated annual service cost.

Step 5 Construct a block diagram and fault tree for the new design shown in Figure 3.43. Compare the cost in Step 4 to the estimated annual service cost estimated from the new designs incorporating the FMEA recommendation of a redundant bulb.

Worksheet

The estimated occurrence of the failure mode base on the historical component failure rate (See Figure 3.42):

Power Cord (0.02) or Motor (0.01)..... Elect. subsystem (0.0298)*

Bulb (0.10) .... Lighting subsystem (0.10)

Switch (0.01) or Contact (0.02) .... Mech. subsystem (0.0298)

* Probability of occurrence of failure in electric subsystem:
$P(0.02)+P(0.01)-P(0.02)P(0.01)= 0.0298$

now

The estimated occurrence of the failure mode (series system):

Electrical (A)		Lighting (B)		Mechanical (C)	
subsystem	or	subsystem	or	subsystem	
(0.0298)		(0.1)		(0.0298)	$= 0.15284 \approx 0.153$

*Note: The probability of the failure mode occurring, provided the three subsystems are independent, can be calculated in two steps... Step 1: $P(A)+P(B)-P(A)P(B)= P(X)$ and Step 2: $P(X)+P(C)-P(X)P(C) = 0.153$

now

The estimated service cost or failure cost:

Failure rate (0.15284)	x	Annual production (50,000)	x	Service charge ($75.00)	=	**$573,150.00**

Failure Modes and Effects Analysis

The estimated occurrence of the failure mode base on the recommendation (See Figure 3.43)

Power Cord (0.02) or Motor (0.01)...... Elect. subsystem (0.0298)

Bulb (0.01) .... Lighting subsystem (0.01)

Switch (0.01) or Contact (0.02) .... Mech. subsystem (0.0298)

now

The estimated occurrence of the failure mode (series system):

Electrical (A) subsystem (0.0298)	or	Lighting (B) subsystem (0.01)	or	Mechanical (C) subsystem (0.0298)	=	0.06813

* Note: The joint probability of a failure occurring in the first bulb and the second bulb can be calculated ... P(0.10) x P(0.10) = 0.01

now

The estimated warranty service cost of the current design:

Failure rate (0.15284)	x	Annual production (50,000)	x	Service charge ($75.00)	=	**$573,150.00**

adding

Estimated warranty cost of the current design $573,150.00

152

Conclusions:

Implementing the FMEA recommendation of designing-in a stand-by bulb will cost the organization:

$ 10,000.00
$ 3,500.00
$ 150,000.00
$ 163,500.00 + estimated warranty service cost for the proposed design change ($255,487.50*) $418,987.50

*0.06813 X 50,000 X $75.00 = $255,487.50

The estimated service cost without
implementing the FMEA
recommendation $573,150.00

Difference $154,162.50

Implementing this FMEA recommendations is estimated, based on historical design quality, to result in an annual cost savings of one hundred fifty four thousand one hundred sixty-two dollars and fifty cents.

Failure Modes and Effects Analysis

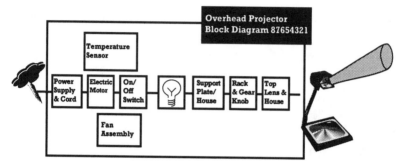

Figure xx

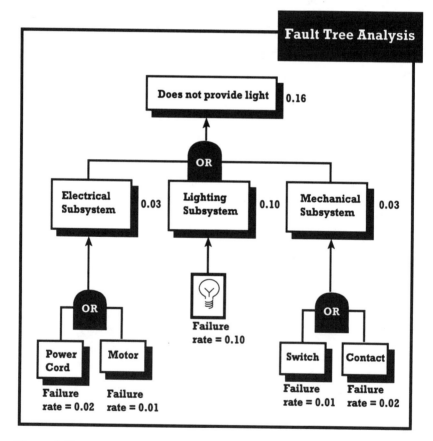

Figure 3.42

154

FMEA REVISION

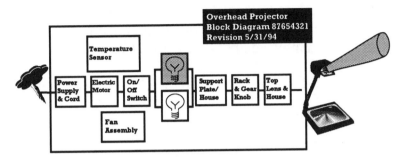

Figure xx

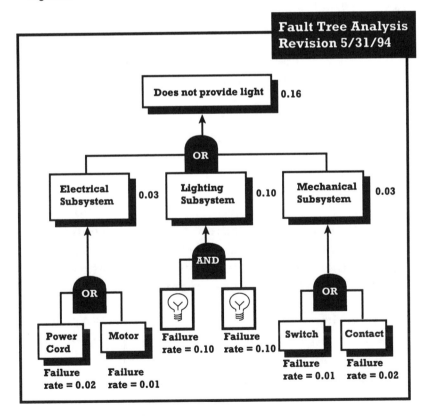

Figure 3.43

Failure Modes and Effects Analysis

Summary

Heading ... The FMEA Heading must include all pertinent information that will allow the team and the subsequent readers to identify the subject matter, what activities or documents will be effected, who is responsible for the development and maintenance of the FMEA and the dates.

Functions ... The first column in the FMEA, Functions, must identify all the things that this design, process or service is supposed to do. A complete list of the functions/ requirements are defined in the following four specifications 1) Engineering specifications, 2) Reliability specifications, 3) Quality specifications and 4) Customer specifications.

Failure Modes ... The second column in the FMEA, Failure Modes, defines how the design, process or service could fail to perform these functions. Remember the question asked in this column is, How could it fail? not if it will fail. This question is asked in a subsequent column, titled Occurrence.

Effects ... The third column in the FMEA, Effects, describes the consequences of each failure modes. It is extremely important to capture the experiences of the end user. Try to experience these effects through the customer's senses; otherwise, the subsequent severity rating of these effects is likely to be underestimated.

Severity ... The fourth column in the FMEA, Severity, asks, How bad are the consequences of the preceding effects resulting from the failure modes? Remember that the measure of "how bad" is based on 1) safety and 2) cost. It is common practice to assign "special consideration" status to high severity ratings where the corresponding effects will place the customer's safety at risk or generate tremendous failure cost.

Causes ... The fifth column in the FMEA, Causes, identifies all the reasons why the failure mode can occur. Recall that many events can contribute to a failure mode; however, as suggested in the Pareto principle, many of these causes are very small contributors and just a few causes are major contributors, referred to as "root causes," and should be identified in the FMEA.

Occurrence ... The sixth column in the FMEA, Occurrences, asks the question, How often is the failure mode or cause likely to happen? This estimate can be based on the collective experience of the team or historical data from similar designs and is commonly rated on a scale from 1 through 10.

Controls ... The seventh column in the FMEA, Controls, describes the existing procedures or equipment that is in place to detect or prevent failure modes from being transferred downstream or to the subsequent customers. Examples of these controls are Design Reviews, laboratory checks, test plans or automated inspection equipment.

Detection ... The eighth column in the FMEA form, Detection, estimates the chance that the failure mode will be delivered to the subsequent customers and is typically rated on a scale from 1 through 10.

It is important to understand the two distinct definitions of detections used in FMEA. 1) The detection in this column is defines as detecting a failure modes before it reaches the customer. 2) The detection used in the Recommendations column is defined as the ability of the customer to detect the failure mode before the effects of the failure mode occur.

Recommendations ... The ninth column in the FMEA, Recommendations, identifies the actions required to address the failure modes identified in the FMEA. These recommendations must be cost-effective and should have a high degree of permanency. In other words, all recommendations should result in quality and reliability benefits to the customer and the supplier that exceed the total implementation cost of these recommendations. Also, the human behavioral aspects must be considered in these recommendations to assess the "degree of permanency." It is possible to develop a solution to a problem that cannot or will not be implemented in a day-to-day basis.

Status ... The last column in the FMEA, Status, has been added to assure that all recommendations are cost-effective and feasible before they are actually approved. Separate task or studies can be assigned to individual FMEA team members to verify or demonstrate this for the high risk recommendations.

The Example/Exercise on the overhead projector demonstrates how each of these elements are developed for an actual FMEA application. The objective of the Example/ Exercise is to address many of the obstacles and questions that often do not surface during FMEA lectures or in the reading.

Chapter Four:
Interpreting the FMEA

Traditional Interpretation

Some of the traditional approaches/guidelines for reading and interpretation the completed FMEA include:

1. establishing the priorities using the RPNs, Risk Priority Numbers, for decision making.

2. a ridged strategic sequence for addressing the failure modes.

These two guidelines, commonly found in many of the recognized company and professional society workbooks, have both advantages and disadvantages. This section will be dedicated to understanding the pros and cons for each of these guidelines. New methods/developments designed to enhance the traditional interpretation of FMEA by exploiting the advantages of the existing guidelines and eliminating the disadvantages of the existing guidelines will be demonstrated in examples throughout this section and in the subsequent sections of this book.

Guideline 1. Prioritize using the RPN for decision making.

This guideline suggests that the higher Risk Priority Numbers warrant first consideration for analysis and resource allocation for improvement; or more directly stated: the team must begin working on the failure modes that have the higher RPNs. In recent years, many companies have added qualifiers to this guideline that include focusing on high severity numbers and high occurrence numbers along with high RPNs. This is an improvement for identifying the most important problems and resolving them more effectively and efficiently. Unfortunately, all of these guidelines continue to include the RPNs in the interpretation allowing the opportunity for the FMEA team to

Failure Modes and Effects Analysis

focus its improvement efforts on a failure mode that may be less critical than the quality, reliability and safety of other failure modes with lower Risk Priority Numbers.

For example, three failure modes A, B and C were identified in an FMEA with the following severity, occurrence, detection and Risk Priority Numbers:

Failure Modes	Severity (1 - 10)	Occurrence (1 - 10)	Detection (1 - 10)	RPN
A	4	5	10	200
B	4	8	2	64
C	9	2	1	18

The RPN strategy can be interpreted to imply that the team first investigate failure mode A and allocate most of the resources toward reducing the RPN of failure mode A. What would you work on or investigate first? A, B, or C?

Failure mode A has the highest RPN; however, the occurrence of failure mode B and the severity of failure mode C must be considered before failure mode A. Let's apply this example in a more personal context (from the customer's perspective) to see if you agree:

You have been completely satisfied with, even enthusiastic about, the current product and are committed to purchasing next year's design. The design responsible engineer informs you of the three potential failure modes listed were identified in this new design. The engineer also explained that due to a business decision that it is only possible to fix two of the three failure modes.

As the ultimate customer or end user of this new design, which failure mode will you recommend that the engineer work on? A, B or C?

As an internal customer of the design engineer responsible for the day-to-day production which failure mode would you suggest that the organization investigate first? A, B or C?

Referencing the ranking scales provided in the preceding section, failure modes B and C are likely to generate extremely high failure cost if not resolved. Failure mode A is likely to incur moderate appraisal cost if resolved; however, it will not compare to the failure cost resulting from failure modes B or C.

If you selected failure modes B and C as the two failure modes to investigation for subsequent resolution, it is apparent to you that minimizing the severity of a failure mode or reducing the occurrence of a failure modes are "proactive" by nature opposed to improving the detection which is "reactive" by nature. (See Figure 4.1)

Proactive vs. Reactive Approach

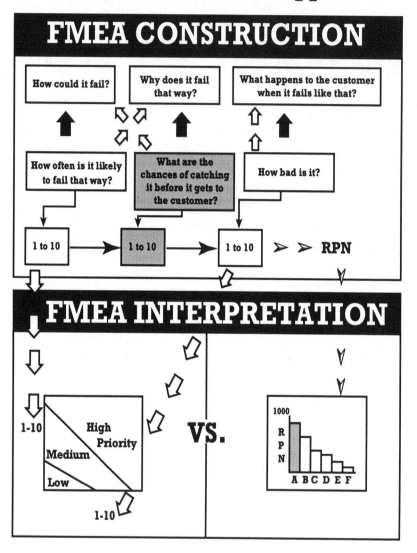

Figure 4.1

Figure 4.1, shown on the previous page, depicts two approaches for:

◊   constructing FMEAs.

◊   interpreting FMEAs.

The two approaches for constructing FMEAs were defined in the preceding section. The two approaches for interpreting FMEAs are compared below as a continuation of Guideline 1.

Failure Modes	Severity (1 - 10)	Occurrence (1 - 10)	Detection (1 - 10)	RPN
A	4	5	10	200
B	4	8	2	64
C	9	2	1	18

As previously stated, the *traditional approach* suggests, strictly based on the highest RPNs, that the top two failure modes are A and B.

A Proactive Interpretation

The *new approach*, Area Chart, (shown in Figure 4.2) suggests, strictly based on severity and occurrence, that the top two failure modes are B and C.

Adding qualifiers, stating that in addition to selecting the highest RPNs the team should look for high severity numbers and high occurrence numbers, supports this new graphical approach for interpreting FMEA. The graphical approach allows a "proactive" interpretation of FMEA compared to the RPN which is a mixture of "proactive" and

Failure Modes and Effects Analysis

"reactive" interpretation. An application of the graphical approach uses the severity numbers and the occurrence numbers for interpreting or selecting the most important failure modes. The detection numbers are not used for the interpretation; however, this number may be used later in the analysis if sufficient proactive gains are not possible.

Before the organization allocates resources to improve detection, all opportunities for reducing the occurrence and minimizing the effects of the failure modes should be considered.

Three regions are depicted in the Area Chart in Figure 4.2:

◊ High Priority

◊ Medium Priority

◊ Low Priority

These regions are define by the organization's policy on FMEA. For example, some organizations state that a severity number of 9 or greater shall be designated as a control characteristic or high priority. A similar statement can be made about the lower limit for occurrence. If we establish 10 as the lower limit for occurrence we can define the high-priority region of the Area Chart by drawing a line beginning at the 10 on the occurrence axis and ending at 9 on the severity axis. The medium-priority region of this chart can be defined similarly by specifying lower limits for medium priority.

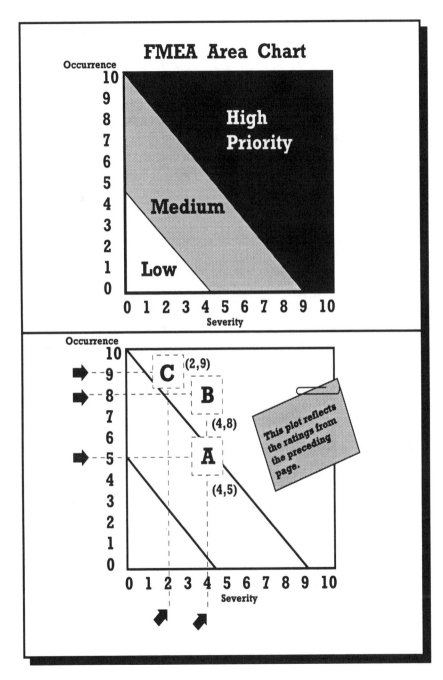

Figure 4.2

Strategies for addressing the failure modes

Guideline 2. A ridged strategy for addressing the failure modes.

A very common strategy, found in many of the FMEA training manuals, for addressing the failure modes implies a ridged sequence for high numbers shown below:

1st.   Reduce the severity.

2nd.   Reduce the occurrence.

3rd.   Improve the detection.

It is suggested that the first two choices, reducing severity and reducing occurrence, may be interchangeable depending on the situation. However, improving the detection should always be considered last of these three options. It should be noted that if it is possible to eliminate the occurrence then the severity becomes a moot point; however, reducing the severity will not have the same impact on occurrence. For this reason an argument can be made for the sequence below:

1st.   Eliminate the occurrence.

2nd.   Reduce the severity.

3rd.   Reduce the occurrence.

4th.   Improve the detection.

There is one more action that can be added to this group. Recall that there are two distinct types of detections that apply to Failure Modes and Effects Analysis: Detection 1 — detecting a failure mode/cause before it is delivered to the customer and Detection 2 — designing-in detection for the customer during use to allow the customer to avert a catastrophic failure. The strategy now expands to:

5th.   Provide a means of detection for the customer during use.

Again, arguments can be made that certain situations justify interchanging the first action and the second action of the sequence for FMEA interpretation provided above. The fourth and the fifth actions should always be considered as the last of these options.

Guideline 3. Controlling Upstream vs. the Forgiving Principle.

Controlling upstream or Robust Design, making the design insensitive to variation, is a sound strategy and makes good sense. It can be very expensive, and it may not always provide the best cost-effective solution for achieving the quality/reliability targets set be the organization.

Some examples of Robust Design are:

a) Spring designs

b) Flexible ends on metal tubing

a) A very practical common application of springs for Robust Design is found in the battery storage compartments of electronic equipment. The battery storage compartment is insensitive to the variation in battery length and stack up tolerances. It is important to note that Robust Design may not be the best strategy for all situations.

b) For example, a design engineer could design flexible ends on ridged metal tubing. This would make this tubing insensitive to connecting parts variation, reference location variation and dimensional tube variation, such as length.

However, flexible tubing is likely to be much more expensive. A simple and very common example of Robust Design is found in connecting tubing/pipes for the plumbing industry. The home owner has a choice of both ridged tubing/pipe and flexible tubing/pipe when purchasing materials. The home owner who is more susceptible to construction project variation is likely to buy the robust flexible tubing. The plumber or construction professional is likely to purchase the ridged tubing and save material cost by exploiting the "forgiving" principle. It is possible to achieve quality and reliability using Robust Design or the forgiving principle.

Take the shortest, least expensive path toward problem prevention or problem resolution.

Potential problems are often resolved effectively and efficiently through design changes/action; however, it may be possible to resolve potential design problems more efficiently and on occasion more effectively with a manufacturing change/action. The latter is also referred to as "forgiving downstream" opposed to the "controlling upstream" Robust Design.

Applications of the strategies above are demonstrated using examples/exercise in the remainder of this section. Variations in the FMEA forms and differences in the method of constructing FMEAs are also demonstrated in these examples/exercises. The reader is asked to interpret each FMEA and assess the corresponding recommendations to determine if the recommendations are addressing the most important concerns based on the reader's interpretation. The answers are given in the FMEA revisions on the subsequent page.

Design FMEA

Subsystem ___ **Example 1** ___
Model ___
Outside Supplier Affected: Yes ___ No ___

Engineer ___
FMEA Date Original ___ Revision ___
Schedule Production Release ___

Part Name Part Number	Part Function	Failure Mode	Effect of Failure	Cause of Failure	O	S	D	RPN	Recommendation Corrective Actions
Capacitor #123456	Shuts dwn. speed control if the break switch fails	Shorts out	Uncontrolled accel.	Defects in dielectric Loose connection	2	10	10	160	Relocate capacitor in the circuit to cause this to fail safe. The capacitor can only fail when the engine stops.
Atmosphere Valve	Vents vacuum for smooth throttle function	Leaks	Vehicle surging	Deformed spring	2	2	3	12	Increase the spring wire diameter.

How would you interpret this FMEA?
What is the concern?
Is the concern being addressed?

Figure 4.3

Failure Modes and Effects Analysis

The most important concern depicted in the FMEA in Figure 4.3 is the severity of the effects from the potential failure mode "Shorts Out." The effects of not being able to control the acceleration will place the customer's safety at high risk. Other expletives come to mind that describe the seriousness of not being able to control the speed of the car! These descriptions can be translated into "most important concern." Now that the most important concern has been identified, the question becomes, Do the recommendations in the last column address the concern? In this case, yes. The design engineer can relocate the capacitor in the circuit to control the condition of failure. By changing its location, this component can only fail after the vehicle engine is turned off. This is an example of changing the design to reduce the severity number. To reduce the severity this design change must produce more desirable effects of the potential failure modes. All customers agree that not stopping the vehicle is less desirable that not starting the vehicle. Surprisingly, the difference of opinion is in the severity rating of not starting the vehicle. Informal surveys conducted during seminars shows that vehicle designers and manufacturers rate this severity low, a median of two. On the other hand, the drivers/customers who were not car designers or manufacturers rated the severity of not starting the vehicle much higher, a median of eight. Eight will be used for the example in Figure 4.4.

Excluding the customer's input from the FMEA is likely to result in both an incomplete list of the effect and low estimates of the severity numbers.

Changing the effects has reduced the severity number from a ten down to an eight. A severity number of eight is still considered high; therefore, additional action may be required to try to cost-effectively reduce the occurrence and try to provide some warning to the driver before the capacitor shorts out and strands the driver. Once the team has satisfactorily addressed all of the most important concerns identified in the FMEA, they can then focus on the less important concerns. For example, the atmosphere valve can leak. Looking at the corresponding ratings, it is apparent that reducing any of these numbers will result in a small improvement. Should the team consider improvement for this failure modes?

On occasion the team may decide not to review RPNs below a certain number in an effort to save time. For example, when using scales that range from one through ten, the product of the three scales can equal one thousand. A policy that would ignore RPNs below twenty seems reasonable when RPNs can approach one thousand. There are two disadvantages to this policy: 1) the most obvious being it is possible to have a severity of ten for an RPN below twenty and 2) some of the recommendations that will results in benefits that exceed the implementation cost will not be identified. For example, from Figure 4.4 reducing the occurrence of leaks in the atmosphere valve from a two down to a one can be a very small improvement. What if the total cost, time and money, to increase this spring wire diameter is less than the benefits in the expected quality and reliability improvement?

Design FMEA

Subsystem **Example 1 Answer** Engineer _____
Model _____ FMEA Date Original _____
Outside Supplier Affected: Yes ____ No ____ Schedule Production Release _____ Revision **1 of 1**

Part Name Part Number	Part Function	Failure Mode	Effect of Failure	Cause of Failure	O	S	D	RPN	Recommendation Corrective Actions
Capacitor #123456	Shuts dwn. speed control if the break switch fails	Shorts out	~~Uncontrolled accel~~ ~~System will not turn off~~ Cannot start vechicle	Defects in dielectric Loose connection	2	~~10~~	10	160	Relocate capacitor in the circuit to cause this to fail safe. The capacitor can only fail when the engine stops.
Atmosphere Valve	Vents vacuum for smooth throttle function	Leaks	Vechicle surging	Deformed spring	~~2~~ 1	2	3	12	Increase the spring wire diameter.

Additional recommendations?

Should the team work on this?

2 or 8

Figure 4.4

174

Example 2

How would you interpret the FMEA in Figure 4.5? What are the concerns and are the recommendations addressing these concerns? If not, what would you proposed as a member of this FMEA team?

There two concerns identified in the FMEA: The first concern, shown in Figure 4.6, is the severity of nine for the effect "no drive." The initial recommendation is to strengthen the plastic lever by making it thicker and adding ribs. This will only reduce the occurrence of the lever breaking; however, when it does break the severity will remain a nine for that driver. The team should first investigate the possibility of reducing the severity number. If it is not possible to do so, the detection should be improved in addition to strengthening the plastic lever.

The other concern depicted in Figure 4.6 is the high occurrence number of eight for the failure mode "Loose Fit." The recommendation of installing a load sensor to detect loose fits and sort them out does not address the occurrence. The same amount of loose fits will be created, only now the organization will have a more accurate count of how many loose fits are being created when this load sensor is installed. Reallocating the resource for detecting and sorting out loose fits toward reducing the occurrence of making loose fits will result in a greater payback to the organization in failure cost savings such as less rework, less scrap, less warranty and higher customer satisfaction. This strategy is also a better guarantee of preventing the problem from getting to the customers.

Design FMEA

Subsystem _____ **Example 2**

Model _____

Outside Supplier Affected: Yes ___ No ___

Engineer _____

FMEA Date Original _____ Revision _____

Schedule Production Release _____

Part Name Part Number	Part Function	Failure Mode	Effect of Failure	Cause of Failure	O	S	D	RPN	Recommendation Corrective Actions
Lever assembly	Links the manual valve and park valve to the transmission	Plastic lever breaks	No drive Lock in park	Overload when disengaging Inferior plastic Low temp. Damaged during installation	3	9	7	189	Increase lever thickness Add ribs to lever design
		Loose fit	Cannot detect position	Thermal set of the plastic	8	4	8	256	Install load sensor to automatically detect and sort out the loose fits

How would you interpret this FMEA? What is the concern? Is the concern being addressed?

Figure 4.5

Design FMEA

Example 2 Answer

Subsystem _____
Model _____
Outside Supplier Affected: Yes ___ No ___

Engineer _____
FMEA Date Original _____ Revision __1 of 1__
Schedule Production Release _____

Part Name Part Number	Part Function	Failure Mode	Effect of Failure	Cause of Failure	O	S	D	RPN	Recommendation Corrective Actions
Lever assembly	Links the manual valve and park valve to the transmission	Plastic lever breaks	No drive Lock in park	Overload when disengaging	3 1	9 ?	7	189 63	Increase lever thickness
				Inferior plastic					
				Low temp.					Add ribs to lever design
				Damaged during installation					
		Loose fit	Cannot detect position	Thermal set of the plastic	8 ?	4	6 4	256 128	Install load sensor to automatically detect and sort out the loose fits

Figure 4.6

Failure Modes and Effects Analysis

Example 2a

In example 2a, a comparison is made between the two approaches for constructing the FMEA. (Refer to top of Figure 4.1.)

◊ Rating the occurrence and the detection of the **failure mode** (Figure 4.6).

◊ Rating the occurrence and the detection of each individual **causes** contributing to the failure mode (Figure 4.7).

Both of these approaches for constructing the FMEA are acceptable; in fact, they will provide the same answers. The decision as to which approach to use should be made at the discretion of the team, or the organization may elect to define one approach as the preferred approach. Both of these approaches must be defined in the organization's FMEA manual/handbook and subsequent internal training must provide a clear understanding of these two approaches. This has been a common misunderstanding; a question frequently asked during the FMEA implementation is, Are we rating the failure mode or the causes?

The failure modes are the ultimate target of all the recommendations in the FMEA. Before you can make any improvement to the potential failure mode you must first, identify the root causes and second, make improvement to these causes. We can depict these two approaches for constructing the FMEA by looking at how each approach bridges this relationship between the failure mode and the causes.

Rating the occurrence and the detection of the failure mode:

The analysis begins by estimating how often the actual failure mode happens and how easy or difficult it is to detect this failure mode. If this failure mode has a high severity number or a high detection number, a detailed investigation to determine the root causes should be the next step. This investigation will eventually require the team to measure or quantify the contribution of each cause to the failure mode, as well as a measure of the improvement made of each cause to estimate the reduction for the failure mode rating. The sequence is:

Step 1.   Rate the failure mode.

Step 2.   Measure the contribution of the causes.

Step 3.   Quantify the improvement of the causes.

Step 4.   Correlate the improvement in the causes to the failure mode (Reference Figure 3.12).

Step 5.   Assign the new rating to the failure mode.

Rating the occurrence and the detection of the individual causes:

For this approach, each cause of the failure mode is rated and recorded in the respective Occurrence column and Detection column. This approach is much *more dependent on defining the relationship* between these causes and the failure mode. This sequence is:

Step 1.   Correlate the causes to the failure mode (Figure 3.12).

Step 2.   Rate the causes.

Step 3.   Quantify the improvement in the causes.

Step 4.   Correlate this improvement to the failure mode.

Design FMEA

Subsystem _____ **Example 2 a**
Model _____
Outside Supplier Affected: Yes _____ No _____

Engi...
Rating the occurrence and the individual causes
Rating of the individual ... detection of the...

Part Name Part Number	Part Function	Failure Mode	Effect of Failure	Cause of Failure	O	S	D	RPN	Recommendation Corrective Actions
Lever assembly	Links the manual valve and park valve to the trans-mission	Plastic lever breaks	No drive Lock in park	Overload when dis-engaging	1	9	7	63	Increasing lever thickness and adding ribs to lever design reduces the occurrence of both causes
				Inferior plastic	1	9	1	9	
				Low temp.	4̶ 2	9	1	3̶6̶ 18	
				Damaged during installation	8̶ 3	9	6	4̶3̶2̶ 162	
		Loose fit	Cannot detect position	Thermal set of the plastic	8̶ 4	4	8	2̶5̶6̶ 128	Add elements to the base material to minimize thermal set over a wider range of temperatures

Figure 4.7

Example 3

A different FMEA form is shown in next example (Figures 4.8 and 4.9). The columns used with each of the three scales, Severity, Occurrence and Detection, have been relocated in the form and positioned directly behind the column to which that scale is being applied. For example, the Severity column follows the Effects column suggesting that the Severity Scale ratings apply to the effects; this is true for all cases. The Occurrence column and the Detection column follow the Cause column suggesting that the Occurrence Scale and Detection Scale ratings apply to the causes not the failure modes.

Another modification to this form is the addition of a column for identifying control characteristics. Recall that some FMEA manuals suggest that control characteristics must be identified for all failure modes that produce effects that exceed a minimum severity number. This number is commonly set at nine when using a scale from one through ten. For the example in the following pages we have identified three failure modes that are expected to produce effects that result in severity rating of nine or ten. It is suggested that the team identify these three effects with a symbol. This symbol can be removed if the team is successful in reducing these effects and the rating for the new effect is less than nine. However, on occasion technology may not exist or it may not be feasible from a cost standpoint (quality and reliability do have a point of diminishing return) to reduce the severity number. If this is the case, the following actions are suggested:

1. Identify or link the effect to a measurable design feature. (Reference Figure 3.12)

For the example in Figure 4.9 the effect "water damage" has a severity rating of nine. An investigation revealed that excessive torque on the valve demonstrated a strong relationship to water leaks. This applied torque can be measure during the manufacturing process.

2. Transfer this symbol to the design print torque specification.

3. Invest resources in reducing the occurrence and improving the detection of out-of-torque.

4. Establish a repeatable and reproducible measurement system.

5. Identify the optimum point in the operation to measure the applied torque.

6. Review the above steps in the Process FMEA.

7. Incorporate a detailed strategy of how to monitor this design feature/control characteristic in the manufacturing control plans.

8. Include this item in the product audit program.

9. Reference these control characteristics in the Quality Contract portion of the Purchase Agreements.

Design/Process FMEA

Subsystem _____ **Example 3   Page 1 of 2**
Model _____
Outside Supplier Affected: Yes _____ No _____
FMEA Date Original _____ Revision _____

Reference Documents
Assembly Print M2000
Quality Contract 17540
Mfg. Control Plans 22
Process Flow Charts 2
Audit Program 313
Reliability Test Plan 00

Team Members
Engr. Bill Klanney
Purch. Raquel Gonzales
Qlty. Art Vasaloski
Mfg. Bob Moore
SQE Brandon Holiday
Rel. Andy Flowers

Part Name / Part Number	Part Function	Failure Mode	Effect of Failure	S	Cause of Failure	O	D	RPN	Recommendation Corrective Actions
Water faucet UK-TAP	Deliver water	Will not deliver hot water	Cannot clean	7	- Damage valve - Blocked	2 3	~~6~~ 1 5	~~84~~ 14 105	Revise process to install valve at final operation
		Will not deliver cold water	Cannot drink	9	Same as above				
	Restrict flow	Low pressure	Cannot use the sprayer	4	Valve out of position	1	3	12	
	Mix the hot/cold water	Cannot control the temperature	Too cold ~~Too hot~~	6 ~~8~~	- Seal missing - Seal torn	~~5~~ 2 ~~9~~ 3	~~8~~ 4 10	~~240~~ 48 ~~720~~ 300	Mold the seal on the assembly as one part Upgrade seal tear strength with higher grade material
		Water will be too hot	1st deg. burns	10		3			

Control Characteristic

Often rephrasing the effect can change the severity number

Figure 4.8

Design/~~Process~~-FMEA

Example 3 Page 2 of 2

Subsystem _____
Model _____
Outside Supplier Affected: Yes _____ No _____
FMEA Date Original _____ Revision _____

Reference Documents

Assembly Print M2000
Quality Contract 17540
Mfg. Control Plans 22
Process Flow Charts 2
Audit Program 313
Reliability Test Plan 00

Team Members

Engr. Bill Klanney
Purch. Raquel Gonzales
Qlty. Art Vasaloski
Mfg. Bob Moore
SQE Brandon Holiday
Rel. Andy Flowers

Part Name Part Number	Part Function	Failure Mode	Effect of Failure	S	Cause of Failure	O	D	RPN	Recommendation Corrective Actions
Water faucet UK-TAP	Rinse off dishes	Will not spray	Hard to clean dishes	4	Molding material blocks hose	~~3~~ 1	~~6~~ 2	~~72~~ 8	Add hose cleaning operation in the process / Add rinse check
	Contain water at source	Water leaks	High water bills	8	- Dmg. washer - Loose assembly	4 2	7 5	224 80	An engineering study is being conducted to delete washer from the design (Pending)
		Flooding	Water damage	9	Crack valve from high torque	~~8~~ 5	2	~~144~~ 90	A standard operating procedure (SOP) will define the max. torque specification

Forgive Downstream

Low Degree of Permanency

Control Characteristic

Figure 4.9

Figure 4.9

Two additional points should be noted in this example. The recommendations contained in the FMEA (Figure 4.9) demonstrate the use of the "forgiving principle" and note the concept of "degree of permanency".

Forgiving Downstream and **Degrees of Permanency**

The recommended action "add a hose cleaning operation in the process" was found to be less expensive and more effective than trying to design a hose that would be robust to process contamination. Therefore, the manufacturing engineer agreed to forgive the hose contamination further downstream in the process by adding a hose cleaning operation at the end of the line.

The failure mode, flooding, is caused by excessive torque in the valve during assembly. The team elected to write a standard operating procedure (SOP) specifying the maximum application torque and the torque sequence. This SOP would be a requirement approved by management. Strict adherence to the SOP would be extremely effective in reducing the occurrence of cracked valves and subsequent flooding; but, the recommendation has a low degree of permanency. Degree of permanency is a measure of how effective a solution is or how frequent a procedure is adhered to. Unfortunately, SOPs or procedures are often ignored. Local municipalities have written and posted many procedures (such as the 55 m.p.h. speed limit that few drivers follow) along the highways that are constant reminders of how SOPs have a low degree of permanency even with stiff penalties for ignoring these procedures. Often SOP may be the only feasible option; however, the team should first explore the possibilities of implementing solutions that have high degrees of permanency:

Degree of Permanency	Type of Corrective Action
High Permanency	Full Automation
Medium Permanency	Partial Automation Human Intervention
Low Permanency	Complete Human Intervention

Example 4

The next example depicts the use of the Area Chart for the FMEA interpretation. Recall that the Area Chart allows for a completely proactive interpretations compared to the RPN (crossed out on the form) which is a combination of proactive activities and a reactive activity. This following example, modified for publication, is for a system or system FMEA.

Major revisions were planned to consolidate and expand the current Warranty Reporting, Estimating and Tracking System. The warranty improvement team elected to evaluate these revisions using FMEA. Examples of a portion of this FMEA is shown in Figures 4.10 and 4.11.

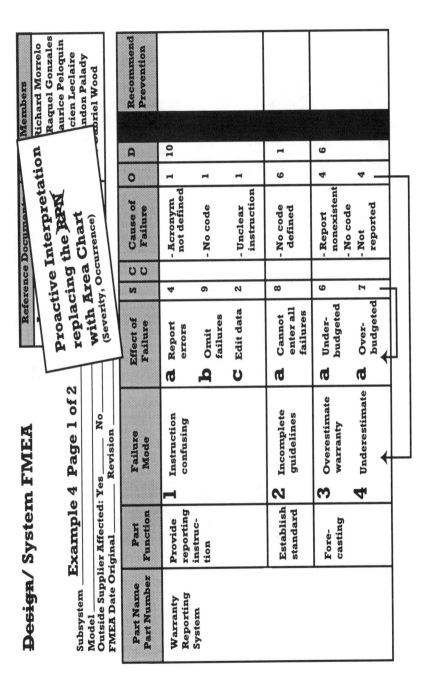

Figure 4.10

Design/System FMEA

Example 4 Page 2 of 2

Subsystem _____
Model _____
Outside Supplier Affected: Yes ____ No ____
FMEA Date Original _____ Revision _____

Reference Document

Members: Richard Morrelo, Raquel Gonzales, Maurice Peloquin, Lucien Leclaire, Landon Palady, Gabriel Wood

Proactive Interpretation replacing the RPN with Area Chart (Severity, Occurrence)

Part Name Part Number	Part Function	Failure Mode	Effect of Failure	S	C C	Cause of Failure	O	D		Recommend Prevention
Warranty Reporting System	Provide input for the reliability program	5 Misleading information	a Lose sales	9		- Report vague	1	10		
			b Wrong target	6		- No code	0	2		
		6 No input	a Miss targets	7		- Data not ??????	2	2		
	Establish volumes	7 Low volume	a Recompute cost	4		- No code - Unclear instruction	5	5		
		8 High volume	a Recompute cost	5		- Wrong instruction	1	5		
	Retrieve	9 Retrieve partial data	a Low estimate	8		- Insufficient memory	9	1		

Figure 4.11

188

Constructing the Area Chart

The Area Chart, shown in Figure 4.12, is constructed using the two proactive rating scales, occurrence and severity, from the FMEA and assigning alphanumeric codes to the failure modes and their effects. The importance of the failure modes were defined based on their location in the Area Chart.

Recall the following steps are used for constructing the Area Chart and plotting the data contained in the FMEA forms (Example 4 from the preceding pages):

Step 1.

Construct equal length scales placing the Severity Scale on the horizontal axis and the Occurrence Scale on the vertical axis. For this example, the range is one through ten; for the actual case study, a range of one through five was used for the scales because the nature of these ratings did not require a wide range and the team began to experience difficulty in using the scale of ten.

Step 2.

Define the regions within the Area Chart. The first region (high priority) was established using a guideline for the organization's FMEA manual. This guideline states that all effects that results in a severity number of nine or greater shall be designated as a control characteristic. Therefore, the team established the beginning point of the high-priority boundary at nine on the Severity Scale. They extended this policy to the Occurrence Scale and established the ending point of this boundary at ten on the Occurrence Scale, thus defining the high-priority region. The team defined the medium-priority region by arbitrarily drawing a line from the number four in the Severity Scale to the

Failure Modes and Effects Analysis

number five on the Occurrence Scale. All points falling between these two lines shall be considered medium priority or addressed after all of the high-priority failure modes have been investigated. The lower right angle of the Area Chart defines the low-priority region. *These boundaries should be consistent with the organization's quality policy and procedures.*

Step 3.

All the failure modes are coded numerically. The corresponding effects for each failure mode are coded alphabetically. Each failure mode/effect is identified by an unique alphanumeric code. The coordinates for each alphanumeric code are obtained by identifying the associated severity rating for each effect and the associated occurrence rating for each failure mode. For example the first failure mode in the FMEA, shown in Example 4, Figure 4.11, "misleading information" has two effects:

Failure Mode (Occurrence)	Effect (Severity)	Coordinates
Misleading Information (1)	Loss sales (9)	(9,1)
	Wrong target (6)	(6,1)

Note: The convention for writing Cartesian coordinates is (x,y). That is the first number denotes the horizontal scale or the x-axis, and the second number denotes the vertical scale or the y-axis. For this example, it is only required to recognize the Severity Scale and the Occurrence Scale and note the correct number sequence.

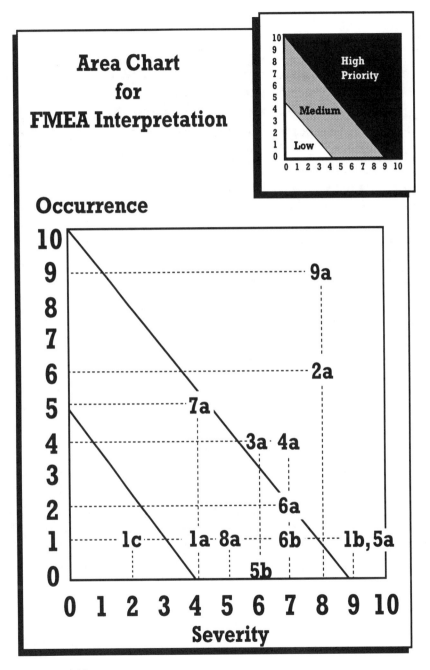

Figure 4.12

Failure Modes and Effects Analysis

Example 5

This example, shown in Figure 4.13, represents one component of a precision pin machining process. The majority of the problems are historically generated in the grinding operations section of the process. This Manufacturing PFMEA begins immediately after the cutting operations, which precede the grinding operations, and ends with the last grinding operation. The approached used was to rate the occurrence of the causes leading to the process failure modes and to rate the detection of the causes leading to the process failure modes. What observations can you make about this PFMEA?

One observation that can be made in the PFMEA revision, shown in Figure 4.14, is that the existing process controls are completely reliant on inspection. One strategy will be to convert many of these reactive process controls to proactive actions when selecting the recommendations to address the concerns identified in the this PFMEA. The top four concerns that were identified are: "length out- of-specification," "diameter not round," "burrs" and "side face taper." The engineer suggested that it would be feasible to design in an adjustable pin retainer that would eliminate the effect "cannot assemble." This recommendation would allow the team to reduce the severity number of nine. Other new effects that are less severe were introduced with an estimated severity of five. Unfortunately, the team had no feasible way of reducing the severity of not being able to match the bearings, and no additional improvement could be made toward reducing the occurrence or the detection of these causes that contribute to this effects. Some other recommendations were made that were expected to reduce the occurrence of "uneven feed rate of the table" and "gear travel." Improving chemistry of the emulsion flow of the coolant used in the grinding process and demagnetizing the bar stock were expected to reduce the occurrence of both of these causes leading to side face taper and burrs. The last recommendation was to implement statistical control charts on a temporary basis because sufficient reduction in some of the severity numbers and some of the occurrence numbers were not attainable. The two control charts were expected to produce slight reduction in some of the occurrence number, depending on how they were implemented by the manufacturing personnel. Slight reduction in some of the detection numbers was also anticipated.

Failure Modes and Effects Analysis

Description [Design/Process/Service]
(Example 5)
Machining precision pins
process (grinding line - G2)

Department/Team Member
Design — Darryle V.
Mfg — Jerry X.
Rel — Carl G.
Qlty — Lou H.
Supl — Peter B.
Cust — Alex T.

Affected Documents
ES _____
PFD — PFDG2
CP — Control Plan CPG2
Contract _____
Survey _____
Test Plan _____

Page 1 of 2
Original _____
Date _____
Approvals

Process Functions	Process Failure Modes	Effects of Failure	S	Causes	O	Process Controls	D	Recommendations
Face grinding	- Side face taper	- Assembly loose fits	6	Jerky feed rate of table	7	- Spot check - Visual inspection	6	
	- Burrs	- Tight fits	8	Worn wheel	3	- Audit	4	
	- Length out-of-spec.	- Cannot assemble	9	Movement in positive stop	2	- Audit	3	
	- Diameter not round	- Cannot match the bearings	9	Tolerance stack up	1	- Inspect and sort	1	
	- Surface scratches	- Excessive wear in mating	7	Worn guide plate	2	- Inspect and replace	3	
		- Reduce contact	4	Insufficient pressure	4	- Inspect and adjust	3	

What would you recommend for addressing these process concerns?

Figure 4.13

Failure Modes and Effects Analysis

Page **2** of **2**

Description [Design/Process/Service]
(Example 5)
Machining precision pins
process (grinding line - G2)

Department/Team Member
Design — Darryle V.
Mfg — Jerry X
Rel —
Qlty —
Supl —
Cust — Alex T.

Revision

Affected Documents
ES — PFD — PFDG2
PFD — CP — Control Plan CPG2
CP — Contract —
Contract — Survey —
Survey — Test Plan —
Original —
Date —
Approvals —

100% Reactive!

Process Functions	Process Failure Modes	Effects of Failure	S	Causes	O	Process Controls		Recommendations
Face grinding	- Side face taper	- Assembly loose fits	6	Jerky feed rate of table	7 / 2	- Spot check - Visual inspection	6 / 3	- Improve the emulsion flow - Demagnetize the bar stock
	- Burrs	- Tight fits	8	Worn wheel	3 / 1	- Audit	4	
	- Length out-of-spec	- Cannot assemble -Mat'l cost - Tool wear	9 / 5	Movement in positive stop	2	- Audit	3	- Design-in an adjustable pin retainer to compensate for out-of-spec. pin length
	- Diameter not round	- Cannot match the bearings	9	Tolerance stack up	1	- Inspect and sort	1	- Implement Statistical Process Control (SPC): • U-chart for all grinding defects • Multi-variable chart for dia./length
	- Surface scratches	- Excessive wear in mating	7	Worn guide plate	2 / 2	- Inspect and replace	3 / 1	
		- Reduce contact	4	Insufficient pressure	4 / 3	- Inspect and adjust	3 / 1	

Figure 4.14

Failure Modes and Effects Analysis

Example 6

Figure 4.15 represents a Service Process FMEA. PFMEA would be a powerful tool for all the other service industries that are competing for customer loyalty. A number of organizations in the service section have accumulated an impressive number of quality plaques reflecting Deming's Fourteen Points, Crosby's absolutes and the individual organizations' quality statements, all of which are posted in building lobbies; unfortunately, many of these organizations have yet to enter the awareness stage of quality and reliability. This is due in part to the fact that many of the publications and much of the training in the quality and reliability sciences has been directed to design and manufacturing. This is changing, and it is expected that the service section will eventually apply many of these quality and reliability tools that can be directly transferred or modified to aid in the prevention and resolution of service problems.

This observation should be taken constructively. Effective implementation of FMEA, as well as many of the other quality tools, can provide any service organization with the means, an almost unfair advantage, of accelerating their quality and reliability level of its services, thus, capturing a majority of the market as loyal customers. Some areas where Service PFMEA may provide tremendous opportunities for an organization's future growth through continuous improvement and subsequent customer satisfaction leading to customer loyalty include:

◊ The hotel industry

◊ The airline industry

◊ Health care providers

◊ Rental companies

All of these industries have established procedures on how to deliver a service. In other words, all of these industries have processes.

A process is a sequence of repeatable events.

Within these processes there exists opportunity for improvement. This improvement can come about reactively or proactively. All companies cannot survive indefinitely when operating in the reactive mode!

Process FMEA

Example 6

Subsystem ___ Car Dealership Repair Process ___
Model ___
Outside Supplier Affected: Yes ___ No ___

FMEA Date Original ___ Revision ___
Schedule Production Release ___

Page 1 of Many

Process Operation	Process Function	Failure Mode	Effect of Failure	Cause of Failure	O	S	D	RPN	Recommendation Corrective Actions
Describing the required repairs	Service write-up								
	Identifying warranty coverage								
	Informing recall items								
Problem Evaluation	Problem verification								
	Cost and time estimates								
	Approval from customer								

What contributions can you add to this PFMEA from the customer's perspective?

Figure 4.15

Summary

The Risk Priority Number (RPN) is the traditional method used to interpret or read the completed FMEA. The RPN is the product of the severity rating, the occurrence rating and the detection rating. Reducing the severity number and the occurrence number is proactive. Reducing the detection number is reactive. The RPN combines both proactive actions and reactive actions; therefore, using the RPN to determine the most important failure modes can be misleading.

A new approach introduced for interpreting FMEA, the Area Chart enables a completely proactive interpretation. This chart has three distinct regions: a low-priority region, a medium-priority region and a high-priority region. The failure modes that are plotted in the high-priority region of the chart are considered to be the most important failure modes.

The Area Chart is constructed by assigning the Severity Scale to the horizontal axis and the Occurrence Scale to the vertical axis. The occurrence rating of the failure modes and the severity rating of the effect resulting from the failure modes serve as the coordinates plotted on the Area Chart.

Recall that the interpretation of the FMEA is dependent on the approach used for the FMEA construction. One approach is to assign occurrence ratings to the failure modes, while another approach is to assign occurrence ratings to the causes leading to the failure mode. The choice as to which approach to use should be at the discretion of the FMEA team.

Strategies suggested for addressing the failure modes

Failure Modes and Effects Analysis

in some of the existing FMEA handbooks are ridged and may not provide the best sequence for this task. Flexibility in these strategies is identified in this section. The first consideration for all strategies should place all proactive actions ahead of any reactive actions. Resources should be allocated for improving detection when sufficient reduction in the severity rating and the occurrence rating is not possible.

Two principles that should be applied to these strategies for addressing the important failure modes are 1) the forgiving downstream principle and 2) the controlling upstream principle. This will allow the development team to achieve the design quality and reliability goals expediently and cost-effectively.

The first design FMEA (Example 1) depicts the approach of rating the occurrence of the failure modes. This example also emphasis the problems of not soliciting the customer's input and provides considerations for addressing small Risk Priority Numbers should the team elect to continue using the RPN for interpretation.

The second design FMEA (Example 2) also used the approach of rating the occurrence of the failure modes. This example points out some problems associate with varying the strategy sequence for addressing the failure modes.

Example 2a compares the other approach, rating the occurrence of the causes leading to the failure mode. This example demonstrates that although the approaches are different the recommendations for improvement are the same for both Example 2 and Example 2a.

The third example demonstrates the use of a different FMEA form. This form includes additional information in the heading for linking the FMEA to other documents in the company and an additional column for identifying critical characteristics. This example also demonstrates the application of the "forgiving downstream" principle and the concept of "permanency."

The fourth example, a system FMEA, demonstrates the proactive interpretation using the Area Chart. The failure modes are assigned a number and the corresponding effects are assigned letters giving each "failure mode/effect" combination a unique alphanumeric code. Each code is then plotted in one of the three regions of the Area Chart which identifies the failure modes as either 1) high priority 2) medium priority or 3) low priority.

Strategies were given for constructing an FMEA Area Chart. The Severity Scale and the Occurrence Scale make up the coordinates for the chart. The three regions of the chart are defined by each organization's specifics FMEA policies. These boundaries may change. Remember the boundaries are set by the organization, the policies, the industry standard and the customer requirements.

The fifth and sixth examples represent PFMEAs. The fifth example depicts a part or component of a manufacturing process FMEA and some of the strategies from developing and analyzing this PFMEA. The sixth and last example is intended to create an awareness of possible applications for service FMEAs and as an exercise for internal FMEA training. The reader may agree that application in the area identified in this example may be a good place to begin and certainly has sufficient opportunities for process improvement.

Chapter Five:
Implementation
Strategies

Managing the FMEA efforts and keeping the team focused

There is some resistance to FMEA in many of the organizations today. This is due in part to the current practices of managing the development of the FMEA and strategies of deploying this task throughout the organization. One misconception demonstrated when developing FMEA is that FMEA is treated as an added, almost separate, activity to the engineering tasks. Ironically, the FMEA is the engineer's thought process! In fact, it is the thought process of everyone in the organization who works to design, build and provide a defect-free product. The FMEA simply structures this thinking by coordinating everyone's thoughts and capturing them on paper.

This relationship between the design, the engineer and the FMEA can be illustrated using an analogy that relates human life to one reliability concept: the reliability "bathtub curve" shown in Figure 5.1.

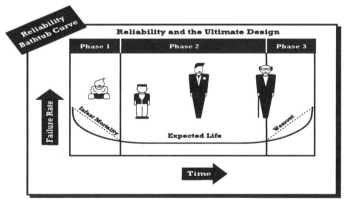

Figure 5.1

This curve depicts the three phases of a design's life: 1) infant mortality 2) expected life and 3) wearout.

Failure Modes and Effects Analysis

As mentioned earlier, FMEA is a diary of the design during conception when the engineer anticipates all potential failure modes that could develop during any of these three phases and what actions are required to prevent them. (See Figure 5.2).

Failure Mode Sources

Phase 1	Phase 2	Phase 3
✓ Design Quality	✓ Design Quality	✓ Design Quality
✓ Mfg. Quality	✓ Mfg. Quality	✓ Mfg. Quality
	✓ User Habits	
	✓ Environment	
Infant Mortality	Expected Life	Wearout

Figure 5.2

Ideally, this diary will contain all the potential failure modes and the most efficient prevention actions and prevention planning to ensure the best possible design life. Similarly, the planning of human life should begin with good prenatal care and subsequent planning for the other phases of human life. The best plans are accomplished as a team: the parents, family physicians, schools and churches. Everyone would acknowledge that this task requires a genuine team effort; however, parents are responsible for ensuring the quality of life. For industry, the task of developing a design and the FMEA should be a team effort; however, the engineer is responsible for this task. The engineer responsible for the concept should not attempt to delegate the responsibility of the FMEA to another discipline within the organization.

Would you delegate the responsibility of bringing up your children to your neighbor?

Another critical task for effectively managing an FMEA is ensuring representation and input from all the groups that influence the final design/process or are affected by the design, the process or the service. One major barrier to this task is the traditional boundaries between departments that exist in large organizations. On occasion departmental goals are established that suboptimize the final quality and reliability of the design. In reality this may not change; however, a well represented and a well managed FMEA team is the best protection an organization has against suboptimizing the final design quality for specific departmental goals. Finally, the most common suggestion for improving the management of current FMEA projects is to include the suppliers in the FMEA development especially in the early stages for the suppliers that are providing the raw materials and the critical components or subassemblies. Input from the suppliers, as well as the customers, can be obtained without divulging or risking the transfer of proprietary company technical information. An FMEA team member from the organization can act as a liaison to present the requirements and explanations of specific areas of the design to the suppliers. The team can also select a representative or employ the services of marketing and the field service engineers to obtain the effects and severity ratings for the potential failure modes experienced by the customers. A Copyright Agreement, shown in Figure 2.3 in section two of this book, is also suggested for joint FMEA development projects. An FMEA is incomplete without this input from the customers and suppliers. Assuring that this input is considered as part of the FMEA development by effectively yet discriminately including the suppliers and the customers as active FMEA team members is an important and formidable task of managing any FMEA project.

Developing internal procedures will assist in managing FMEA projects as well as developing FMEA within the organization. Some of the fundamental elements of FMEA procedures are show in Figure 5.3.

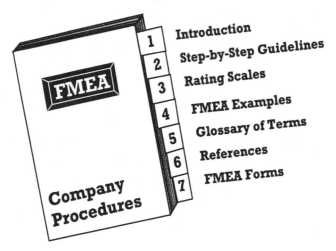

Figure 5.3

1) FMEA procedures should begin with a brief introduction explaining what this technique is, how this technique is applied and why FMEAs must be developed.

2) These procedures should also include clear, understandable, step- by-step guidelines on how to plan, construct and interpret FMEAs. *These guidelines must be tested by actual implementation and debugged before being released as a company document!* There is evidence that this does not happen some of the time.

3) As previously discussed, another element of these procedures should provide rating scales that reflect the nature of the organization's products (Severity Scale), the organization's quality history (Occurrence Scale) and the manufacturing systems (Detection Scale) that exist within the organization.

4) Adding concise and direct examples to these procedures will help convey the ideas and concepts. Examples that are vague and have not been tested are likely to add confusion.

5) Unfortunately, the terminology in many sciences, including the quality and reliability sciences, has not been standardized. A glossary defining all the key terminology can be attached to the appendix of all procedures to ensure that everyone understands and speaks the same language.

6) Finally references should be identified in the internal procedures to allow the reader to research or access additional details on supporting concepts or techniques. The actual procedures should not be cluttered with details that belong in reference materials. The more clutter, the better the chance of masking the intentions of the procedures.

7) Variations of the FMEA forms should also be provide. It is suggested that greater success in the application of FMEA can be expected by allowing each team in the organization some flexibility in the approach and in the interpretation of FMEA. As in the objective of this book ...

Failure Modes and Effects Analysis

... It is not practical to tell one how to apply FMEA because each organization or project within that organization may be unique; however, once the team obtains a thorough sound understanding of FMEA then this team will be in a position to select the most effective and efficient of these variations of FMEA that will guarantee success in these programs for the specific organization.

Reducing the development cost and improving FMEA effectiveness

One of the major costs of developing FMEAs is meetings! There is a widespread thinking that an effective FMEA must be developed entirely as a team and during team meetings. This approach not only greatly increases the cost, it also jeopardizes the integrity of the information in the FMEA.

It *is not* advisable to sequester the FMEA team in frequent meetings with excessive durations. While team meetings are necessary, much of the FMEA can and should be developed outside the meetings, not requiring all the team members to complete each specific task of the FMEA. For example, Figure 5.4 depicts a flow chart of a development pattern for an FMEA.

Figure 5.4

Failure Modes and Effects Analysis

The following approach is recommended for developing an FMEA:

Step 1) An Introductory Meeting
The FMEA team leader provides an overview of the FMEA project to the team members, outlining the overall development program schedule, defining the objectives and FMEA guidelines, and assigning the roles and responsibilities of the each team member.

Step 1a)
FMEA training is provide to team members who have not been exposed to FMEA or who have requested this training.

Step 2) Completing the FMEA Prerequisites
The engineer mails an overview of the design requirements along with overviews of the reliability requirements, quality specifications/quality history and customer requirements to the FMEA team. The engineer can also identify the majority of the design functions and the potential failure modes on the FMEA and distributes copies of this partially developed FMEA to the team members along with the specification overviews. The team is then asked to identify other design functions and potential failure modes that were not identified by the engineer.

An interim meeting may be required to review the results of these forms that team members have returned to the engineer or to answer specific questions on some of the specifications. After this is completed satisfactorily, the team is assigned the task of filling out the remainder of the FMEA and submitting them to the engineer for review.

Step 3) Reviewing the Results
The results from Step Two are reviewed in a team meeting. Any open issues that cannot be resolved in the

meeting are assigned for future investigation to obtain an objective conclusion.

The FMEA team is likely to loop through the first and second steps a number of times before agreeing that it is time to build the first prototypes. FMEA is an iterative process, as shown previously in Figure 5.4. Remember, FMEA is constantly changing, undergoing updates to assess and reflect continuous improvement of the design over time.

A new development, the "FMEA Input Form," shown in Figure 5.5, introduced in this book will further reduce the FMEA development cost and improve the effectiveness of the FMEA .

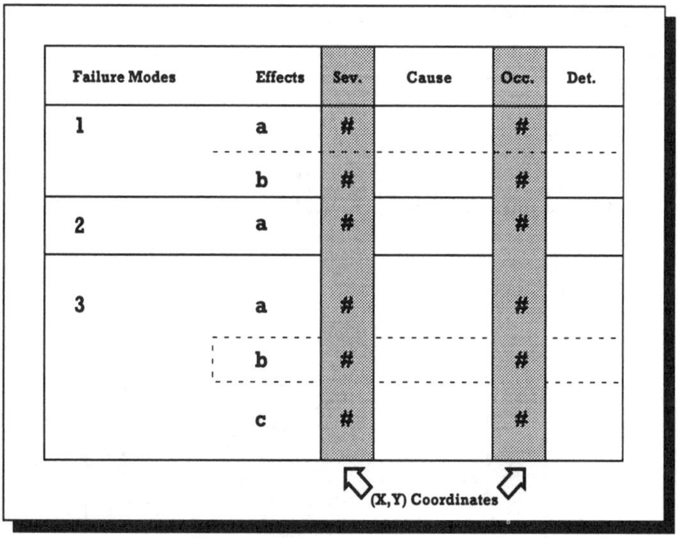

Figure 5.5

This form makes FMEA accessible to more individuals that influence the final design, process or service. A cover letter along with the other overview documentation is attached to these forms and the complete package is forwarded to FMEA team members that may be located in different buildings, cities, states or countries. This form removes the barrier that has traditionally prevented other non-centrally located disciplines in the organization from participating in the FMEA due to travel cost and time constraints.

The FMEA Input Form shown in Figure 5.5 makes use of an alphanumeric coding system. A number is assigned to each failure mode and letters are then assigned to the corresponding effects of each failure mode. This provides each "failure mode/effect" combination with a unique alphanumeric code. The occurrence rating of the failure modes and the severity rating of the effect provide the coordinates for plotting each failure mode/effect in the Area Chart as shown in Figure 5.6.

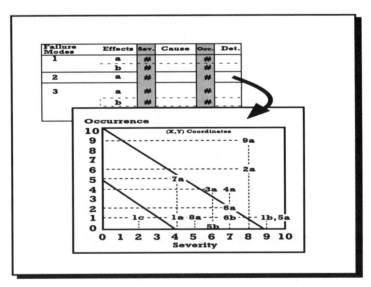

Figure 5.6

As demonstrated, the Area Chart provides a summary of the 1) most important failure modes, high priority 2) the medium-priority failure modes and 3) the low-priority failure modes, as well as providing a completely proactive interpretation of the FMEA.

Leveraging recommendations for maximum improvement

A common problem shared by all organizations is the allocation of a fixed amount of resources to an unlimited amount of opportunities for improvement, i.e. problems. This problem is addressed with the introduction of another new development, the FMEA Screening Matrix, shown in Figure 5.7.

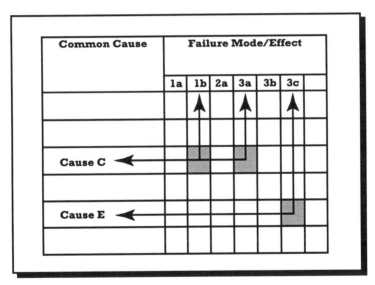

Figure 5.7

All of the failure mode/effect codes located in the "high priority" region of the Area Chart are transferred to the top row of the screening matrix. All the causes from the original FMEA Input Forms are then transferred into the column on the right side of the screening matrix. A check

Failure Modes and Effects Analysis

mark is placed at the intersection of the row and column whenever one of these causes is identified as a contributor to that high-priority failure mode. The completion of this task will identify a few "Key Causes" by an accumulation of check marks in a few of these rows. Allocating the resources or high leveraging these few Key Causes is likely to generate improvement in a majority of the high-priority failure modes.

SAE Technical Paper # 940884 "Restoring The Effectiveness of FMEA"

The first applications of these new developments in FMEA [1) the FMEA Input Form 2) the FMEA Area Interpretation Chart and 3) the High Leverage Screening Matrix] were originally demonstrated in a 1994 Ford System FMEA project to redesign the Powertrain Warranty Reporting and Tracking System. The results of this case study were later presented as a technical paper at the 1994 SAE (Society of Automotive Engineers) International Congress in Detroit, Michigan.

Abstract

New developments on the construction and the analysis of Failure Modes and Effects Analysis increase the efficiency of constructing and analyzing FMEAs. These developments also improve the focus on the priorities for achieving the maximum improvements while providing efficient utilization of resources.

These enhancements to the FMEA are accomplished by the introduction of four new developments: 1) an FMEA Input Form 2) an Area Chart for Analysis, competing with the traditional RPNs, 3) a Common Cause Screening Matrix and 4) a Key Cause Summary Chart.

Introduction

The purpose of this paper is twofold: A) To demonstrate these enhancements to the FMEA by providing examples from the completions of a recent administrative application and B) To provide sufficient detail such that a comparison can be made between these new developments and traditional applications in FMEA based on personal experiences.

Failure Modes and Effects Analysis

A few of the common problems associated with the traditional FMEA applications have been identified as: the lack of team participation due to time constraints, missing or partial information due to limited experience, an unclear strategy for improvement and implementation costs that exceed the anticipated benefits.

Scope

This paper addresses the problems encountered during the initial steps of the construction of the FMEA and ends with the recommendations for improvement. It does not address the prerequisites required for FMEA or the considerations for assessing the risk associated with the final recommendations derived from the study. The aforementioned are important considerations for the overall success of this technique; however, they would require considerable text to adequately cover.

New Developments

The increased efficiency and improved focus of the FMEA is accomplished via the introduction of four techniques:

1) An "FMEA Input Form" that reduces the cost and increases the efficiency of the FMEA data collection by simplifying the method in which this data is collected.

2) An "Area Chart" for identifying the Priority Concerns.

3) A "Screening Matrix" that extracts the Key Common Causes of failure. This supplements the use of the traditional Risk Priority Number and allows resources to be applied to the common causes of failure.

4) A "Key Common Cause Summary" to provide an overview of the causes identified by the Screening Matrix and to display opportunities for improvement for failure detection.

To illustrate the effectiveness of these four techniques, excerpts from a recent Ford Motor Company administrative FMEA will be used.

Case Study

A project to improve the Ford Motor Company, Powertrain Operations Warranty Estimating and Reporting System will be used to demonstrate the above concepts. This project was undertaken to improve the system's effectiveness and accuracy by systematically identifying the potential failure modes of this system and subsequently changing the system design to minimize the potential system failures. Objectives for this project were to anticipate the potential failures that will result in the most severe consequences and those potential failures that occur at high frequencies. These high severity and high occurrence failures ("Priority Concerns") where then screened for Key Common Causes. Accomplishing these objectives allowed the team to focus and manage the allocated resources for the most effective Warranty Tracking and Reporting System improvements.

As a first attempt to accomplish these objectives, the Improvement Team elected to construct an administrative FMEA. However, throughout the planning and the development of the FMEA, the Warranty System Improvement Team (Mark Bednarek, Bob Dascenzo, Carlotta Glover, Elise Kapenlanski, Charles Thomas) encountered situations that were not readily applicable to the traditional approach for design and process FMEA. To overcome these

Failure Modes and Effects Analysis

difficulties, the new developments described above were incorporated into this project.

The first step in the FMEA process is to gather information concerning the system's failure modes, effects and causes. Once this information has been gathered, each failure mode/effect is subjectively rated (1 best - 10 worst) for its potential impact to the overall system. Ratings are determined for each of three classifications:

1. Severity

2. Frequency of Occurrence

3. Probability of Detection

Input Form

An FMEA Input Form shown in Figure 5.8 was developed to reduce the time and the cost of getting this input for the FMEA. This form also organizes the data into a format that will input directly into the Area Chart to aid in selecting and prioritizing the concerns.

FMEA Input Form

Failure Modes	Effects	Sev.	Cause	Occ.	Det.
1 Letter of instruction instruction not clear	**A** Receive wrong classification	9	Letter not Complete Wrong code	4	4
	B Must edit data	5	Unknown		
2 Recieve data by engine code only	**A** Cannot generate report	6	Wrong code sys. config.	1	8
	B High estimates	7	Unknown		
3	**A** Low estimates	1	Missing Data	0	10
		X		**Y**	

Figure 5.8

Area Chart

Thirty-nine concerns were identified from the input collected on the FMEA Input Form. By locating each of these concerns on a grid with their severity on the Y-axis and occurrence on the X-axis, the concerns are readily summarized and priorities are more easily assigned. Using this technique, fourteen concerns were identified as High Priority. Each Priority Concern depicted in the Area Chart shown in Figure 5.9 is coded alphanumerically. The letter indicates the potential failure mode while the number indicates the effect from the FMEA Input Form shown previously in the Figure 5.8.

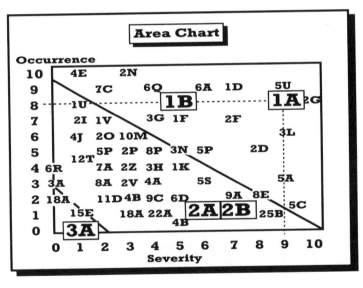

Figure 5.9

Failure Modes and Effects Analysis

For example, the first two codes **1A** and **1B** are plotted on the Area Chart directly from the Input Form:

Failure Mode/ Effect	Number/ Letter	Severity/ Occurrence	Coordinates
Letter of instructions not clear/Receive wrong classification	1A	9/8	9,8
Receive data by engine code only/Cannot generate report	2A	5/8	5,8

Screening Matrix

Once the high-priority concerns had been identified using the Area Chart, a Screening Matrix, shown in Figure 5.10, was constructed by relating the high-priority concerns to their causes. This provides a simple method for identifying the causes which are common to a number of failure modes.

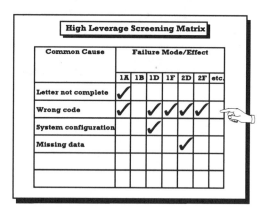

Figure 5.10

Using this approach, causes are listed vertically; failure modes, horizontally and a check mark is placed in each cell where a cause has been identified as a contributor to the failure mode. The rows with the highest frequency of check marks are designated as the "Key Common Causes." This technique serves as an economic model for planning, allowing the Improvement Team to effectively direct solutions to the high leverage causes.

Resolving these four Key Common Causes will provide the most expedient, cost-efficient path toward resolving the majority of the high-priority concerns that were identified in the FMEA Area Chart.

Key Common Cause Summary

While it has been shown that the majority of the allocated resources should be assigned to the four Key Common Causes that were extracted from the Screening Matrix, the detection ratings for each of the Key Common Causes shown in Figure 5.11 can also be included. Traditional FMEA applications suggest that the "Detection" rating should also be used to identify the Priority Concerns (RPN). However, Risk Priority Numbers can produce misleading results. Detection is considered a reactive strategy, as opposed to proactive strategy, such as reducing the severity or reducing the occurrence. Therefore, detection ratings should be considered when sufficient reduction in severity and occurrence is not attainable and improvement in detection is possible.

**Summary
of the
Recommendations**

Addressing the Key Common
Causes listed below is likely to
maximize the improvements in
the majority of the most important
Failure Modes listed in the FMEA:

* Improvement in the instruction
  letter
* Improvement on the selection
  codes
* Flexibility in "reporting by engine"
* Provide equality for all in reporting

Figure 5.11

Improvement Strategy

Once the concerns have been identified, the following
strategy is used to allocate resources. This strategy, shown
in Figure 5.12, seeks to provide complete corrective action
for each concern, rather than a short-term "fix."

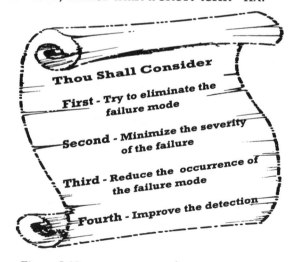

Figure 5.12

Next Steps

Although the concerns identified above are the Key Concerns, Continuous Quality Improvement efforts must be continued to resolve all the concerns identified on the FMEA. However, limitations regarding available resources and costs must be balanced against the number of concerns being addressed at any time.

Since the Key Common Causes identified concern supplier issues, the Improvement Team must next identify what the suppliers need and want to assist them to gain a better understanding and to improve their compliance for entering data into the Warranty Reporting and Estimating System. This next step can be accomplished using the first phase of a Quality Function Deployment (QFD) study. The supplier needs and wants for attacking the four Key Common Causes can be translated into system design requirements via the QFD design matrix. These design requirements can then be considered for the next series of Warranty System improvement changes.

Conclusions

The concepts described above provide a simple method for utilizing the FMEA approach for prioritizing failure modes within the typical business constraints of time, cost and human resources. Implementation of these methods provides a mechanism for efficient utilization of these resources while continually improving quality.

Deploying FMEA inside the organization

Writing mandates making FMEA a requirement and documenting these written policies in all the quality procedures is not sufficient and probably not the best way of deploying the implementation of FMEA throughout the organization and its supplier base. Two suggestions are proposed that will assist in deploying FMEA throughout the organization:

1) An "FMEA Deployment Model"

2) A "Program Development Flow Chart"

The FMEA Deployment Model has four distinct phases and each phase has up to five steps. (See Figure 5.13)

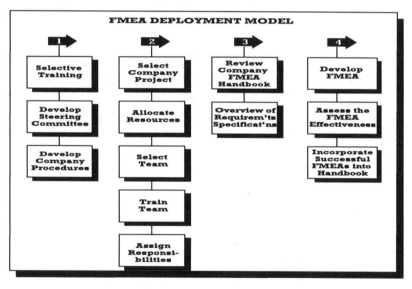

Figure 5.13

The Deployment Model - Phase One:

The first phase of the deployment model contains three actions; selective FMEA training, forming a FMEA steering committee and developing the company FMEA procedures. Initial FMEA training should be conducted for a selected group within the organization. This group will have the responsibility of deciding on or developing the FMEA procedures and policies that are right for the organization. It is important for this group to develop a sound fundamental understanding of FMEA. Some or all group members, along with upper management, should be active participants to a steering committee that will oversee the development of the company's procedures. Individuals from this group may also have the responsibility of coaching upper management on FMEA if they cannot attend the initial training. Company FMEA procedures should reflect the needs of the organization, recall previous suggestions for tailoring the FMEA to the organization. These procedures or FMEA handbook will change as the organization becomes mature in the application of FMEA. Make sure that the procedures can efficiently accept revisions without creating too much confusion and disruption.

Phase Two:

A deployment strategy that can create problems is assigning engineers the task of developing FMEAs for everything they are responsible for. This will cause an overload in the daily schedule and in the manpower, resulting in the generation of many forms containing information of little or no benefit. A review of the warranty, benchmarking studies, risk analysis, other customer feedback and historical quality data bases will provide insight on where to begin the first FMEA projects. Narrowing the FMEA efforts and concentrating the limited resources where they are needed most are likely to result in successful applications with significant payback. Prior to development of the initial FMEAs, the project manager must assure that adequate resources will be available and that FMEA will be fully supported by management and all the other departments. Remember, FMEA *is not* an activity apart from the development and *must not* be treated as an additional assignment to the existing workload!

The third step in this phase is selecting the FMEA team. The project manager must ensure complete representation including input from the suppliers and the customers. This team, only for the initial FMEA project, should attend brief training on the company FMEA procedures/handbook. Following this training the project manager can work with the team to determine individual FMEA team responsibilities for the project.

Phase Three:

The team is now ready to begin the FMEA project. As previously stated, the construction of the FMEA should follow an overview of the requirements and other prerequisites for developing a working level understanding of the design, process or service. This step should not require extensive time; however, allocating as much time as needed for developing this working level understanding is strongly recommended. The accuracy of FMEA construction and all other subsequent tasks are completely dependent on this step. Recall the four requirements or specifications that must be understood and that must be satisfied:

1) The Engineering Specifications/Requirements

2) The Reliability Specifications/Requirements

3) The Quality Specifications/Requirements

4) The Customer Specifications/Requirements

Defining the overall FMEA project, objectives and schedule are other important prerequisites. The project and objective of the FMEA should explicitly inform the team members as to the type of FMEA , the approach, the rating procedures and other general FMEA guidelines that will be followed. The FMEA development schedule must be coordinated with the overall program development schedule and be flexible enough to accommodate a few unexpected developments that often are uncovered when constructing effective FMEAs.

Phase Four:

In this phase, the team has completed all the planning required for successful FMEAs and acquired sufficient resources for the development of the FMEA. The construction of the FMEA begins. As discussed in previous sections of this book, the team can select different approaches for constructing the FMEA, which may require the use of supporting tools from the other sciences and include two techniques for interpreting the FMEA. These decisions should be left to the team's discretion, but the team must reach an agreement on all of these before they begin Phase Four.

Once the FMEA project has been completed and the development program successfully implemented, the team member responsible for updating the FMEA should track the associated program failure costs for a representative amount of time. This failure cost can be compared against historical cost. The difference or the reduction in total failure cost less the FMEA development cost is one of the measured benefits of doing *effective* FMEAs. All successful FMEA developed internal to the organization should be considered for updates as examples to company's FMEA handbook.

The second suggestion proposed will assist in deploying FMEA, as well as all the other development tools, throughout the organization. The "Program Development Flow Chart," shown in Figure 5.14, provides a clear, sequential, overall picture of everything that must occur for program success and most importantly provides a picture of how all the program activities link together. This flow chart is extremely helpful in coordinating the overall program activities, maintaining program focus and minimizing chaos. The program begins with the customer requirements. The customer wants and needs are identified and later linked to the design requirements that will achieve these customer wants and needs. These key design requirements are highlighted in the preliminary draft of the print and used to established the reliability targets. Supplier evaluations and the subsequent selection can occur simultaneously. Once the development team has identified what the customers want or will purchase and the corresponding design features/requirements that will achieve these wants, the best concept for achieving these targets should be selected. All the design alternatives can be evaluated against the design targets using a tool/technique referred to as "Concept Selection." Once the concept has been selected the development team should conduct its first design review, the Preliminary Concept Design Review (PCDR). The objective of this design review is to make sure that the customer requirements are correct, the design features are correct and the best concept has been selected.

The FMEA should begin after all the customer wants and all the design requirements have been identified and the best concepts have been selected and approved in the PCDR. Information extracted from the FMEA can be used to develop the most efficient test plans and assist in the development of an approved part list. Fault tree analysis (FTA) may be required to conduct in-depth investigations on high-risk failure modes identified in the FMEA or to conduct cost/benefits analysis for some of the high-risk recommendations proposed in the FMEA. The results of the FMEAs, FTA, test plans and qualified parts list should be reviewed in a Detail Detail Design Review (DDDR). The objective of this design review is to evaluate and approve critical design features or characteristics, design test points, sample sizes, test conditions, the measurement system and other details required to build and test the design. Prototype development should begin when the DCDR has been completed.

Three series of prototype builds are shown in Figure 5.14. It may not be necessary to build all three series prototypes. Series A prototypes are built in very small quantities, often only one, to demonstrate that the design will actually complete the functions. Series B prototypes are built in small quantities to demonstrate the durability requirements. Finally, Series C prototypes are built in larger quantities and tested under actual field conditions to demonstrate the reliability and the quality targets. Reliability analysis is preformed on the prototype test results. If analysis demonstrated that the design meets the program targets, a Final Design Review is conducted and the design is approved.

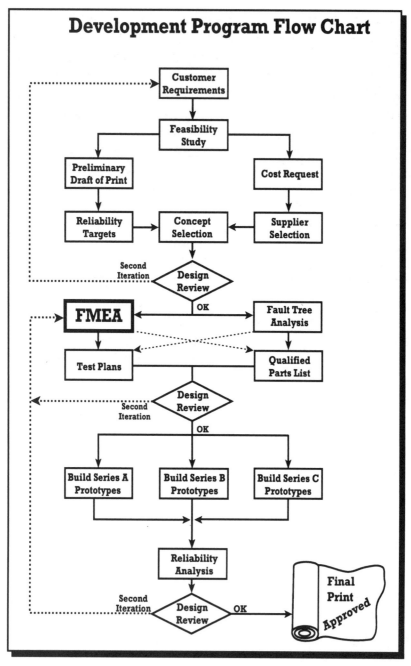

Figure 5.14

Summary

FMEA is the engineer's thought process, in fact it is the thought process of everyone in the company who works toward continuous improvement in his/her specific area.

Failure modes that can occur throughout the three phases of the design life, recall the bathtub curve, should be considered in the FMEA.

Developing a company handbook that is company specific will assist in the deployment of FMEA within the company. Seven suggested elements for this handbook are: 1) an introduction to FMEA, 2) step- by-step guidelines for construction and interpretation, 3) tailoring the rating scales, 4) FMEA examples, 5) a glossary, 6) references and 7) FMEA forms.

New developments for FMEA deployment were introduced for reducing the cost of developing FMEAs and at the same time increasing the effectiveness of the FMEAs. An FMEA *Input Form* can reduce the FMEA meeting time. An *Area Chart* can provide a completely proactive interpretation of the FMEA results and help focus on the opportunities for the highest improvement in quality and reliability. A *Screening Matrix* was introduced for high leveraging the corrective action to maximize the improvement with fewer resources.

The SAE technical paper in this section provides the first FMEA case study using these new developments.

The improvement strategy has four sequential steps:

1) Try to eliminate the potential failure mode.

2) Minimize the severity of the effect resulting from this potential failure mode.

3) Reduce the occurrence of the potential failure mode.

4) Improve the detection of the potential failure mode or causes leading to the potential failure modes

Recall that there are two very different types of detections. The detection referred to in the Detection Scale is defined as: "detecting the problem before it is shipped to the customer." The detection referred to in the Recommendations column is defined as: "detection for the customer that will help the customer avert the potential failure during use."

A deployment model was introduced as a guide for deploying FMEA throughout the organization. This model has four phases with up to five steps in each phase.

A flow chart depicting the overall development program identifies where FMEA fits and how it links to all the other program development tools.

Chapter Six:
FMEA Linkage

FMEA linkage overview

Recall that FMEA is one tool in the reliability tool box, and it is very unlikely that any development or improvement project can be accomplished using only one tool. The effective implementation of FMEA is often dependent on the execution of other supporting quality and reliability tools. FMEA is also an important aspect to many of the quality standards. We think it is important to explore the link between FMEA, the tools and the Quality standards of the ISO 9000 series, in addition to some of the more specific quality standards, such as the cGMP (current Good Manufacturing Practices) administered by the Food and Drug Administration and QSA 9000, Quality System requirements, administered by Chrysler, Ford, and General Motors. It is important to note that the effective execution of these tools are the most expedient, cost-efficient path toward the ultimate goal of all these quality standards: total quality. This path begins with a working level understanding of FMEA and all the supporting tools, and as in the application of tools in all professions, the apprentice is elevated to journeyman status after demonstrating the most efficient use of all the tools of the trade for an number of different projects.

A tool box for the design development program

Some of the tools that may be used to plan the FMEA, support its construction and analyze of the FMEA are:

QFD	*Scatter Plot
Benchmarking	Planned Experiments
Warranty Analysis	*Process Flow Diagram
Pugh Model	Statistical Comparison
R & R Guide	Area Chart
Rate/Rank Matrix	*Check Sheet
*Pareto Chart	Fault Tree Analysis
Block Diagram	*Histogram
Screening Matrix	*Control Chart
*Ishikawa Diagram	Cost/Benefit Studies

* designates the seven QC (Quality Control) tools

Failure Modes and Effects Analysis

Examples are provided in this chapter to demonstrate how the FMEA links to each of these tools. The scope of this section is to raise the awareness of the relationship of these tools to FMEA, not to provide detail information on how to develop and apply each of these tools.

QFD, Quality Function Deployment:

QFD is a tool for identifying what the customers really want and need. These wants and needs are solicited using various marketing survey techniques. Once this "voice of the customer" has been captured, it is used to guide the development of the prototypes and the manufacturing process. Recall, the first question asked in the FMEA form in Figure 3.3 is, What are all the things that this design, process or service is supposed to do to satisfy the customers? QFD is one of the best tools for constructing this column of the FMEA.

Benchmarking:

Benchmarking is often included in the QFD study. In addition to asking the customers what they want and need, the survey often asks how customers rate certain features of the organization's design against the competition. Areas where the organization is lagging behind the competition should serve as input for the first column of the FMEA.

Warranty Analysis:

Warranty data can provide insight on how to prevent potential failures on the next generation designs, as well as target areas for improvement. The warranty reporting system can be one of the most accurate sources for identifying failure modes for the FMEA.

Pugh Model:

Concept selection is often referred to as the Pugh Model. Once all the customer requirements, design requirements and other program mandates have been identified and agreed upon, the design or process concept that will best achieve all of these requirements can be selected using this tool. It is advisable to select and agree on the concept before the developing of the FMEA.

R&R Guide:

The Roles and Responsibility Guide clearly defines what tasks are expected from each team member and when each task is due for the overall program timing. This guide can include team members of the overall program development project, in addition to the FMEA team members. An example of an R&R Guide in shown in Figure 6.1.

R&R Matrix:

The Rating and Ranking Matrix assists in the construction of the three rating scales of the FMEA: Severity, Occurrence and Detection. This matrix manages the ratings from all the FMEA team members by arranging each rating in ascending order and identifying the median number or identifying any outlier or splits. Examples of the R&R Matrix are shown in Figures 2.4 and 3.29.

Pareto Chart:

Pareto charts, summarizing the causes leading to a failure (shown in Figure 3.10) or the types of failures that have occurred historically on past designs, can serve as a reference when developing the Failure Modes column and the Cause column of FMEA. However, as demonstrated earlier, it is not advisable to use Risk Priority Numbers for the interpretation of FMEA.

Failure Modes and Effects Analysis

Roles & Responsibility Guide

Activity	Advanced Planning	Engineering	Purchasing	Reliability	Supplier	Manufacturing	Comments
Customer Requirements	L	S	N/A	R	S	R	Marketing Surveys, Benchmarking Surveys
Feasability Study	L	S	S	S	S	N/A	Establish Program, Program Timing, Rate of Return
Cost request	N/A	R	R	S	L	S	Initiated by Supplier, Defined in Quality Contract
ES Draft	S	L	R	S	L	R	Functional/Dimensional/Physical Requirements, Consult QFD, Concept Selection, Reliability Targets
Select Supplier	N/A	S	R	N/A	L	L	Engineering Recommendations, Purch'g Evaluates & SQE conducts pre-Award Assessment or Provides Supplier History
Reliability Targets	N/A	L	R	S	R	R	Failure Rate, R/1000, Reliability (0-1), MTBF, MMBF
Early Sourcing/Target Agreement	N/A	S	R	S	S	R	Commitment Agreement, Establishing Quality and Reliability Targets, Signed by Ford and Supplier
Concept Selection	S	L	R	S	R	R	Pugh Methods, Consult QFD Customer Wants & Needs and Design Requirem'ts
Preliminary Concept Design Review	R	L	R	R	R	R	Team Review of QFD, Pugh, Program Timing, Program Cost, Gov't Regulations, Industrial Satndards, Safety Issues
FMEA/FTA	S	L	R	S	R	R	Developed as a Team Effort, Include Supplier & Customer Input

L = Lead Role, S = Supporting Role, N/A = Not Applicable, R = Review

Figure 6.1

Block Diagram:

The Block Diagram, shown in Figure 3.22, is a picture of the design. This picture depicts all of the design components or subsystems as rectangles and displays their relationships within the design. When constructing the FMEA, Block Diagrams can serve as references to assure that all functions have been considered in the FMEA. They also are used in assessing recommendations in the FMEA as demonstrated in Figures 3.42 and 3.43.

Screening Matrix:

The Screening Matrix is one of the two new tools introduced in this book and in the 1994 SAE paper #940884 titled <u>Restoring the Effectiveness of FMEA</u>. The Screening Matrix is used to high leverage the corrective actions to extract maximum improvement with fewer resources.

Ishikawa Diagram:

The Ishikawa Diagram, better known as the "Cause and Effect" diagram or the "Fishbone" diagram, shown in Figure 3.11, can be used to structure the FMEA brainstorming activities for the causes leading to the failure modes. This diagram can be used to identify any possible interactions between the causes leading to the failure mode.

Scatter Plots:

Scatter plots depict the relationship of two variables, such as a failure mode and a cause. Scatter plots can also be used to estimate the strength and direction of this relationship. They can be constructed when the FMEA team is either uncertain or is in disagreement as to whether a cause should be investigated or addressed to resolve a failure mode. It is important to note that the scatter plots are the first step in the investigation of a possible relationship. A relationship between two or more variables should be demonstrated using both regression techniques and subsequent test.

Planned Experiments:

Planned experiments are often used to optimize and verify some of the recommendations in the FMEA before these recommendations are implemented on very expensive prototypes. Example of planned experiments include the classical full factorial designs, Taguchi methods and Shainin techniques. Planned experiments help identify which variables in a design or process are the most influential for achieving the desired functions and where to adjust these most influential variables to achieve the best performance of these desired functions.

Process Flow Diagram (PFD):

The PFD is a picture of the process depicting all sequential operations of the process. The PFD serves as a reference for both the Design FMEA and the Process FMEA. The PFD assures that all functions are considered when constructing the first column of the process FMEA. The PFD also assists in identifying the optimum process control points for monitoring control design characteristics and key process parameters identified in both types of FMEAs. An example of a program development process PFD is shown in Figure 5.14, identifying: when the FMEA should begin, control points and how the information flows into and out of the FMEA.

Statistical Comparison:

Often when the FMEA team cannot agree on a median rating for one of the failure modes demonstrated by an "outlier" or a "split" in the R&R Matrix, the team must resort to a more expensive tool to try and establish a possible relationship between a cause and the failure mode. Examples of some of these statistical tools, shown in Figure 3.12, are listed from least expensive to the most expensive:

◊   Correlation Analysis and Scatter Plots

◊   Contingency Table Analysis (CTA)

◊   Screening Experiments (Plackett Burman Designs)

Area Chart:

The Area Chart is one of the two new tools introduced in this book and in the 1994 SAE paper #940884, titled <u>Restoring the Effectiveness of FMEA</u>. The Area Chart enables a completely proactive interpretation of the FMEA.

Check Sheets:

Check Sheets serve as the input form for constructing histograms and control charts. A properly designed check sheet provides information for estimating the occurrence rating in the FMEA. A check sheet has four basic elements that can be expanded on: 1) a heading describing the check sheet topic, 2) a column identifying the subject(s) being inspected, 3) a description of the evaluation criteria and 4) the results of each inspection.

FTA:

Fault Tree Analysis can be used to support the construction of FMEA and to evaluate the recommendations in the FMEA. Recall that FTA may be used to conduct a detailed investigation of failure modes that have very high severity ratings or very high occurrence ratings. The FTA was used in the "Overhead FMEA" example to assist in the deciding to approve or reject the recommendation of designing-in a redundant stand-by bulb. The examples are shown in Figures 3.42 and 3.43.

Histograms:

Histograms are pictures depicting the shape of data. This data can be collected from critical characteristics identified in the design FMEA or key process parameters identified in the process FMEA. The histograms are superimposed on the specifications using the same scale for the "x-axis." Capability formulas can then be used to predict the percentage of the design characteristic or process parameter that will fall outside of or within the specification over a period of time.

Control Charts:

Control charts depict a picture of a process over time, unlike the histogram, which depicts a picture of the process at a single point in time. One use of the control chart is to inform the process operators when the process is preforming or not preforming as designed. This task is accomplished by plotting measurement of a design characteristic or a process parameter at specified intervals in the process. The FMEAs are one of the most accurate sources of selecting the design characteristics and the process parameters of the control chart.

244

Cost/Benefits Studies:

This tool is also used to minimize the risk when making decisions on either approving or rejecting some of the recommendations in the FMEA.

Reference for all of these supporting FMEA quality, reliability and statistical tools are provided in the appendix of this book.

FMEA and other company documentation

Some of the company documents within the organization that are likely to be affected by information extracted from the FMEA and vice versa are the:

- Quality Contract
- Test Plan
- Final Design Print
- Manufacturing Control Plan
- Standard Operating Procedures
- Process Flow Diagram
- Manufacturing Preventive Maintenance Schedule
- Design Repair Procedures and Customer Assembly Instructions

The Quality Contract:

Quality Contracts are extensions of Purchase Agreements. These contracts define all the part numbers, the related requirements and standards, a list of control characteristics, the manufacturing control plans and other information required to assure the quality and reliability of the design, process or service being purchased. Control characteristics identified in the FMEA and the corresponding recommendation in the FMEA should be reflected in the quality contract. All subsequent changes made to the quality contract should be assessed in the FMEA.

The Test Plan:

The Test Plan is a documented strategy of how to test the design to demonstrate that the design will be able to meet each requirements established for the design. Test plans, as in other forms, will vary from company to company; however, they are likely to include many of the common elements shown in Figure 6.2.

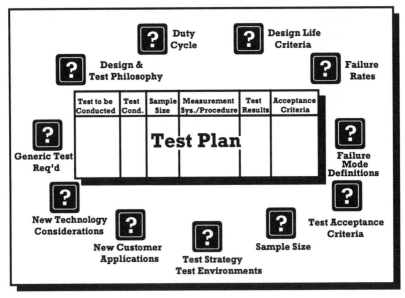

Figure 6.2

Some of the test elements that are linked to the FMEA are shown in Figure 6.3. The design characteristic to be tested, the type of test to be preformed, the number of samples required to demonstrate the requirements at a specified confidence level, and the acceptance criteria are

246

some of the elements contained in the FMEA. For example, failure modes with high severity numbers of nine or ten can be designated as control/critical characteristics. These design characteristics should be transferred to the test plans and tested to ensure that a through assessment of these high risk potential failure modes that were identified in the FMEA as shown in Figure 6.4. Test results may also provide new or unexpected information that can be fed back into the FMEA. The causes identified in the FMEA that lead to the failure modes may provide insight for designing the actual test for inducing test failures. There are two types of testing in a development program: 1) tests to induce failures for identifying weak links 2) failure free tests to demonstrate the design requirements.

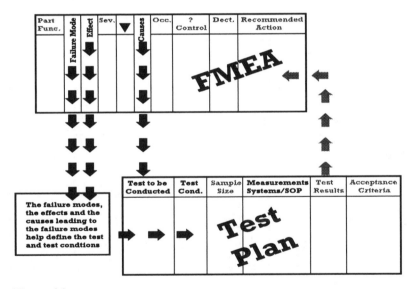

Figure 6.3

Failure Modes and Effects Analysis

Central Air Conditioning System

Function	Failure Modes	S	Effects	S	Causes	O	Controls	D	Recommendation	Status
Pump freon	Low circulation	8	No cooling (hot air)		Piston lock damaged seal	4		10	Upgrade to ceramic seals	
Compress gas	Low pressure	2	Warm air		Seal out of position	2		10		
Circulate freon	No circulation	4	High		Freon leak damaged o-ring	6	Leak rate	5	Add SOP to check unit leak rate every 6 months	
Temperature sensor	Cannot adjust temp.	8	Too cold Too hot		Poor connection	2		7		

Test Plan

Test to be Conducted	Test Cond.	Sample Size	Measurement System	Test Results	Acceptance Criteria
100,000 Cycles	Low oil	15 Seals	Seal fatigue Flex modules	Fatigue cracks Low Flex	No visible min xx KSI
Thermal Cycle	Low temp.	5 Seals	Elongation	Fail min. percent	80 percent minimum
Temp. sensor shock	Vibration	12 Sensors	Tensile test	Pass	Min. tensile after shock load xx PSI

Figure 6.4

The Final Design Print:

The link between the FMEA and the final design print may be obvious by now. Some of the corporate supplier quality programs require that control characteristics be identified in the design prints and monitored during manufacturing using SPC, statistical process control. Implementing SPC for each control characteristic adds cost to the overall manufacturing operation; therefore, the identification of control characteristics and the subsequent SPC should only be executed when absolutely justified. The FMEA is one of the best ways of identifying control characteristics and determining the best means for addressing these characteristics.

For example, a manufacturer of plastic, twist-off cap bottles containing medicine has identified one failure mode of this design as "failure to remove the cap from the bottle." A part of the FMEA reads as follows:

Failure Mode	Effect	Severity	Causes
Cannot remove cap from bottle	Cannot administer medicine	10	- Tolerance stack-up - Excessive assembly torque

The failure mode's effect, "cannot administer medicine," has a severity of ten. As mentioned, some quality programs require that a "control characteristic" is identified and designated for this failure mode and that this designation is identified on the design print. Controls are put in place to monitor this failure mode during manufacture. The question now becomes, How can the engineer link the failure mode to a measurable characteristic in the design print? The answer is found in the Causes column of the FMEA: A tolerance stack-up between the cap's inside threads diameter (ID) and the bottle's outside threads diameter (OD) can cause an interference fit resulting in the failure mode. Both of these diameters were designated as control characteristics and noted as such on the design print, as shown in Figure 6.5. The second cause contributing to the failure mode, excessive assemble torque, will require actions in the manufacturing/assembly process.

The Manufacturing Control Plan:

Using the previous example in Figure 6.5, it can also be seen that special manufacturing actions are often identified from the FMEA. For example, "Excessive assembly torque" contributes to the failure mode "Cannot remove the cap from bottle." Procedures and special instruction for making sure that the proper torque is applied to the bottle cap during assembly to prevent this failure mode, identified in the FMEA, can be developed and posted at the operation. The document used to define these special controls for manufacturing is commonly referred to as the Manufacturing Control Plan.

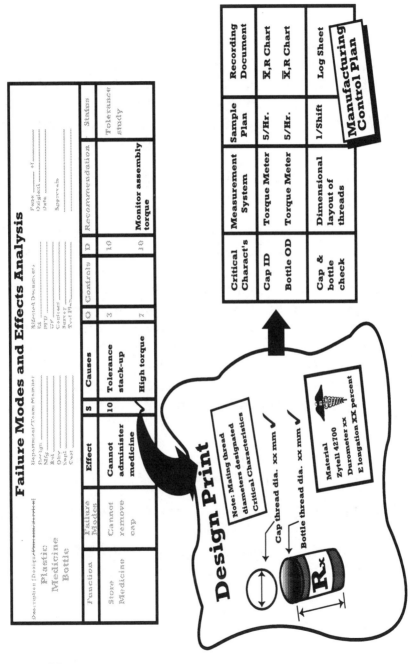

Figure 6.5

Failure Modes and Effects Analysis

SOP, Standard Operating Procedure:

SOPs are extensions of the Manufacturing Control Plan. The Standard Operating Procedure contains the step-by-step details for each item defined in the control plan. SOPs can be used to transfer critical knowledge from the FMEA to the personnel doing the actual manufacturing or assembling or personnel providing the service.

The PFD, Process Flow Diagram:

Knowledge extracted from both the DFMEA and the PFMEA will assist the development team in designing the optimum process the first time, minimizing those very expensive and very stressful surprises that can surface during the initial manufacturing start-up. For example, additional process operations and manufacturing equipment may be required to address high-risk potential failure modes that were identified in the FMEA. The preliminary PFD could be revised to accommodate the extra operations or equipment with addition floor space and other planning tasks can be completed before putting the manufacturing process together.

Why is there plenty of time to do it over, but not enough time to do it right the first time?

The answer is entrenched in our culture and has been our basic training as we entered the work force. Breaking away from this practice is probably the most difficult challenge that most of us face when developing effective FMEAs! The rest is relatively easy.

Preventive Maintenance:

Recall the discussion early in the book on the phrase:

"If it ain't broke, don't fix it" and the fact that preventative maintenance can be a very expensive activity. A thorough analysis of the design or process using the FMEA will help the team decide when the above phrase applies and when it does not apply. This will ensure that preventative maintenance is implemented only when it is required and that the cost of this PM will not exceed any quality, reliability or safety benefits that can result for the customers and the organization.

Design Repair Procedures and Customer Assembly Instructions:

Many failure modes a customer experiences when attempting to repair or assemble the design somehow slip by the technical writers of these repair procedures and assembly instructions. FMEAs can be the best tool for ensuring that the repair procedures and the assembly instructions:

◊ make sense.

◊ are understandable.

◊ really work and are robust to the customer's creativity!

Failure Modes and Effects Analysis

Summary

FMEA is one tool that must be applied with other reliability and quality tools during the design development program.

Quality Function Deployment is one of the tools that can be used to generate functions for the first column in the FMEA. The customer functions are best captured for the FMEA using this planning tool.

Other tools that provide insight for identifying all the functions are benchmarking and historical warranty on similar designs.

The design concept should be selected before developing the FMEA. This will prevent the organization from investing resources in analyzing a concept other than the one it intends to build. Once the concept has been selected the development can begin on the FMEA to identify how to optimize the design.

Two program planning tools that support the development of FMEA by coordinating and tracking the FMEA, as well as all the other supporting activities required to develop a design, are the Process Map and the Roles and Responsibility Guide (R&R Guide). The Process Map depicts the overall development strategy and the R&R Guide identifies all the tasks that are required and the responsible individuals.

Some of the common analytical tools that assist in the development of the FMEA are: Ishikawa Diagrams, Statistical Comparison, Planned Experiments, Fault Tree Analysis and the three new tools introduced in this book 1) the Input Form 2) the Area Chart and 3) the Screening Matrix.

Information extracted from the FMEA may influence other documents within an organization, such as the Quality Contract, Test Plan, Design Print, Manufacturing Control Plan, Standard Operating Procedures, Process Flow Diagram, Preventative Maintenance Schedules and Design Repair/Assembly Procedures.

Appendix A

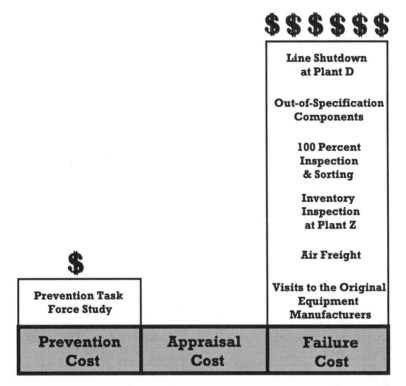

Answer – Exercise 1a

Failure Modes and Effects Analysis

The following FMEA forms were designed specifically for the medical device industry and are aligned with the FDA's cGMP.

Medical Device Design FMEA
Potential Failure Mode and Effects Analysis

Device Component Function	Potential Failure Mode	OCC 1	DET 1	Potential Effect(s) of Failure	SEV	CLASS	Potential Cause(s)/ Mechanism(s) of Failure	Current Device Design Controls	DET 2	Recommended Action Items, Testing, Etc.	Responsibility & Target Date	Action Results			
												Action(s) Taken	SEV	OCC	DET

Reference: Proposed cGMPs, Subpart C – Design Controls, 21 CRF Part 820.30, Section 9(d) Design Verification

SEV (Severity) – CLASS (Classification of Product Defect Involved [C: I, II, III]) – OCC (Occurrence Probability) – DET 1(Ease of Internal Detection) – DET 2 (Ease of Customer Detection)

Prepared for the Food and Drug Administration by: Paul Palady (Practical Applications) & Carl Schwaigholer (ETHICON Inc., A J & J Co.)

Medical Device Process FMEA
Potential Failure Mode and Effects Analysis

Device Process Function & Requirements	Potential Failure Mode	O C C	D E T 1	Potential Effect(s) of Failure	S E V	C L A S S	Potential Cause(s)/ Mechanism(s) of Failure	Current Process Controls	D E T 2	Recommended Action Items, Testing, Etc.	Responsibility & Target Date	Action(s) Taken	Action Results S E V	O C C	D E T

Reference: Proposed cGMPs, Subpart C – Design Controls, 21 CRF Part 820.30, Section 9d) Design Verification

Prepared for the Food and Drug Administration by: Paul Palady (Practical Applications) & Carl Schweighofer (ETHICON Inc., A J &J Co.)

SEV (Severity) – CLASS (Classification of Product Defect Involved [C: I, II, III]) – OCC (Occurrence Probability) – DET 1(Ease of Internal Detection) – DET 2 (Ease of Customer Detection)

Appendix B:
Supporting Reliability & Quality Tools for FMEA Planning, Construction and Analysis

FMEA Planning Tools

Gantt Chart:

The Gantt chart is a traditional tool to depict the overall program timing, establish timing targets for each program task and identify program milestone or any program delays. This chart depicts when the FMEAs should begin and end in the overall design/process development program, in addition to identifying the relationship of other program tasks to the FMEA.

The two components of the Gantt chart are three 1) program timing and 2) program task. The program timing is defined along the horizontal axis, and the program tasks are defined along the vertical axis as shown in Figure 1-A. For this example, the program is expected to take 36 months. The program tasks have been identified on the vertical axis and the "start" and "end" tasks are identified within the rectangle.

The next example shown in Figure 2-A is a modification of the Gantt chart which combines this chart with the Roles and Responsibilities Matrix. Each department or activity has been identified on the vertical axis aligned with the program tasks that they are responsible for. Four phases

Failure Modes and Effects Analysis

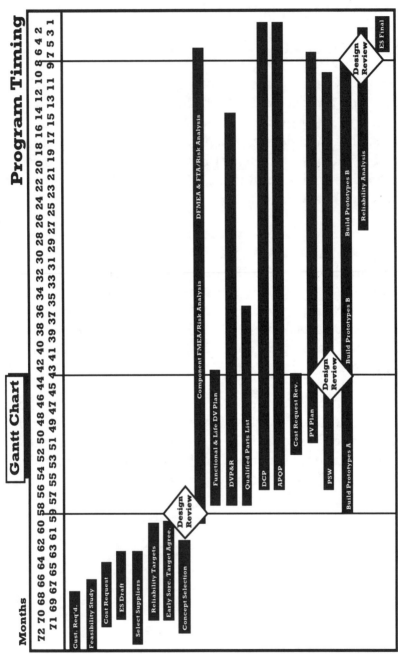

Figure 1-A

Gantt Chart

Timing (Months)	72 Months	43 Months	37 Months	21 Months
	Initial Design Evaluation and Supplier Selection	Initial Design Development	Design Improvement, Verification and Release	Product Readiness

Product Engineering
- System Component Review
- Functional Life & Design Plan
- Supplier Selection Criteria
- Design Reviews
- Functional Design Verification Plan & Testing
- Design Reviews
- Engineering Spec: FINAL
- Failure Analysis, Design Improvement, (FRACAS)
- Reliability Assessment
- Select Supplier
- DVP&R
- DVP&R
- DVP&R
- DVP&R
- PSW Sign-off
- Process Review
- AQP
- AQP
- AQP
- AQP

Purchasing
- CF&R System/Design Trade-off
- Review Engr. Spec. Draft
- Drawing Release
- CMFT Confirmation
- Cost Request
- Tooling Release
- PO Issued

Supplier
- Preliminary Module Targets (Affordable Targets)
- Early Source Workplan & Risk
- Customer Requirements & Functional Specifications
- CPMT Targets
- Supplier Early Sourcing
- Design FMEA (Components)
- Feasibility Study
- Preliminary Design review (In-House)
- Design Reviews
- Engineering Specification DRAFT
- Failure Analysis Reporting System
- Design Verification Plan and Testing
- Design Reviews
- AQP
- AQP
- AQP
- Design Verification Testing
- Process FMEA
- Wellnuft Carven
- PV Testing

Reliability Engineering
- Operational & Environmental Profile
- System Fault Tree and Reliability Predictions
- Select Comparator
- DVP&R Plan
- Reliability Targets
- Trade-off Analysis
- Failure Review and Corrective Action
- Reliability Target Allocation
- System FMEA
- Preliminary Design Review
- Engineering Spec: DRAFT
- System Fault Tree and Reliability Predictions
- Failure Review and Corrective Action
- ES FINAL, Final Print Release

Supplier Quality Engineering
- Customer's Needs & Waste Analysis
- Risk Analysis Procedure
- Schedule and Lead AQP
- Schedule and Lead AQP
- Schedule & Lead AQP
- Existing Supplier Rating
- Form PPQ Team
- Assist on Feasibility
- Review Supplier FMEA
- Review Dynamic Control Plan and Production Planning
- New Supplier Assessment Form
- Initiate Supplier AQP Process
- Engineering Spec. DRAFT
- Review Supplier Process FMEA
- Review Supplier Process, Zero Defect Plan
- ES FINAL
- DCP & Process FMEA
- Approve PSW

Planning
- Customer's Needs & Waste & Program Requirements

Legend:
- ☐ Activities
- ▓ Deliverables

Figure 2-A

267

of the overall program have been identified along the horizontal axis, in addition to the program timing.

Roles and Responsibility Matrix:

The Roles and Responsibility Matrix is a new planning tool developed for the overall design development program that identifies all the groups or individuals participating in the program and their corresponding responsibilities. This matrix can be used to define what tasks are required to complete the programs and which groups or individuals will be accountable for certain tasks. This matrix is useful for establishing the program resources and will prevent disconnects, in addition to eliminating redundancy or duplication of work. An example of a Role and Responsibility Matrix for an FMEA program is shown in Figure 3-A.

Operating Profiles:

The operating profile is a checklist of all the operating functions that the design/process must accomplish. This profile can also include descriptions of the environments that the design/process is expected to perform in. Operating profiles provided added insurance for identifying all of the design/process functions and the subsequent potential failures. An example of an operating procedure is shown in Figure 4-A.

Block Diagrams:

The block diagram is a graphical representation of the components of a design. These diagrams can be used to depict the flow of energy through the components of the design or simply an overview of the arrangement of the individual components or subsystems in the design. Block diagrams assist the design engineer in reviewing the design with the FMEA team and with design reliability analysis. An example of a block diagram is shown in Figure 5-A,

Process Flow Diagram:

The process flow diagram (PFD) is used to depict the sequential step-by-step operations of a process. The process FMEA must begin with a thorough review of the preliminary PFD. This will provide added assurance that necessary operations or critical control points are not overlooked. Revisions to the PFD should be expected from both the design FMEA and the Process FMEA. Linking the PFD to both FMEAs helps prevent process start up changes. Although, process flow diagrams are extremely helpful for planning manufacturing processes, they can be developed for other process such as services and programs. An example of a design development PFD, complete with FMEA operations, is shown in Figure 6-A.

Failure Modes and Effects Analysis

R&R Matrix	Design Concept	Design Development	Design Verification	Product Readiness
Product Engr.	• Develop Block Daigrams • Assist in developing the Reliability Targets or review supplier's reliability • Incorporate the reliability specifications into the functional specifications	• Incorporate the reliability requirements into the DV/PV program • Review specification DRAFT for reliability requirements	• Review and update FRACAS report • Review reliability requirements for feasibility AI-3 and Tooling AI-5 • Review status of overall reliability program	• Review and approve reliability deliverables • Incorporate approved reliability deliverables into final design requirements
Purch.	• Assist in the evaluation of the Supplier's reliability program capabilities • Address reliability requirements cost	• Review Preliminary Module for reliability requirements	• Review reliability issues in cost request • Provide confirmation of reliability deliverables	• Incorporate R&M requirements in the Tooling Release
Supplier	• Submit to Ford Engineering: 1) Reliability Program Plan 2) Reliability Specifications 3) Reliability Targets	• Provide timely reliability program updates to product engineering, such as: FMEAs, test plans, early test results • Provide SQE with Reliability and Maintainability Analysis	• Update failure reporting system and submit to product engineering • Assist SQE in incorporating reliability requirements in the AQP • Provide reliability predictions	• Submit final/approved reliability demonstrations
Reliability Engr.	• Provide support to Engineering, Purchasing and SQE in the Reliability Planning or Assessment of the initial reliability plans	• Provide reliability support to product engineering and the supplier on: Test Planning and Reliability Analysis • Initiate and maintain reliability growth curve	• Provide reliability support in the review of program status, review reliability predictions and make recommendations • Update reliability growth curves • Assist SQE in supplier's R&M	• Provide a review on final reliability assessments and provide recommendation
Supplier Quality Engr.	• Assess the Supplier's Reliability and Maintainability capabilities • Provide support to Purchasing on reliability cost issues	• Review Supplier's Reliability for Manufacturing Program • Coordinate supplier reliability activities with the Ford TQE program	• Coordinate the reliability updates with the supplier's program and the Ford programs • Review reliability cost issues • Coordinate FMEA, DVP&R, R&M and the DCP	• Approve the supplier's R&M plans • Complete on-site assessment or demonstration of the reliability requirements • Review and approve reliability requirements for the PSW, DCP and AQP
Advanced Planning	Identify Customer Requirements and Other Design & Program Requirements			

Figure 3-A

270

Operational and Environmental Profile Coverage

1. Item Under Analysis	Exhaust Manifolds (Part Numbers 9430 and 9431)
2. Application	1.2L 4V V8 Engine, PC49 Big Sedan
3. Model Year	1999
4. Date	4/31/93
5. Analyst	Alfred E. Newman

6. Is the DVP & R opreational parameter coverage adequate?

YES or NO: **NO**

If NO, list operational parameters not covered by the DVP & R:

Operatinal Parameter	Test Offering Best Coverage	Best Test Value	% tile	90 % tile Value
Time at idle	P3-12A Light truck General Durability	110 Hrs.	1	2158 Hrs.
Total time AC clutch engagement	General Durability Route	0.38 Hrs.	1	434 Hrs.
Time at speed > 20% Nmax (1200 RPM)	General Durability Route	802 Hrs.	< 1	2928 Hrs.
Mileage at speed > 70% Nmax (67 MPH)	General Durability Route	13748 Miles	77	37882 Miles
Time of driveline torque > 2655 in-lbs.	General Durability Route	194 Hrs.	28	683 Hrs.

7. Is the DVP & R environmental profile adequate?

YES or NO: **NO**

If NO, list environmental profiles not covered by the DVP & R:

Environmental Profile	Test Offering Best Coverage	Best Test Value	% tile	90 % tile Value
High temperature				120 degrees
Low temperature				-40 degrees
High relative humidity				100 %
Low relative humidity	**Test conducted at ambient values. No special environmental testing is planned.**			5 %
High pressure				32 in. Hg
Low pressure				27 in. Hg
Salt Spray				365 days/year
Wind				50 MPG
Rain				40 in./year
Blowing Snow				72 days/year
Vibration				10,000 Hz

Figure 4-A

271

Failure Modes and Effects Analysis

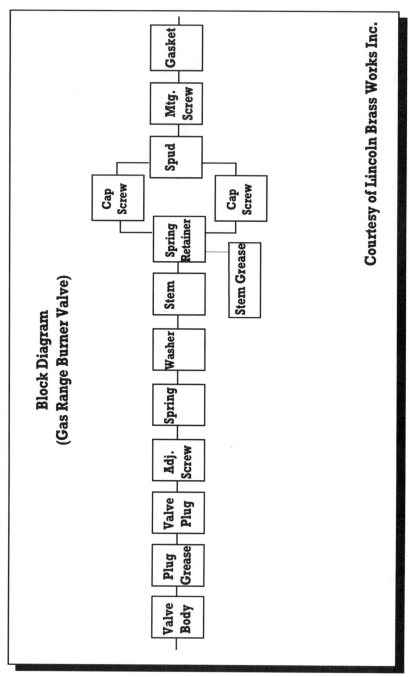

Block Diagram
(Gas Range Burner Valve)

Courtesy of Lincoln Brass Works Inc.

Figure 5-A

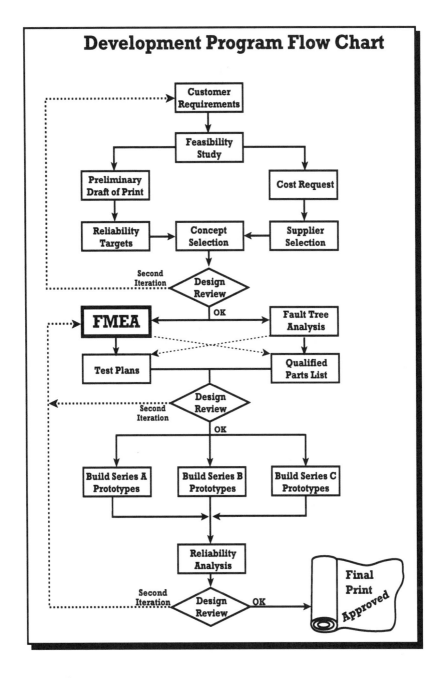

Development Program Flow Chart

```
                    ┌─────────────┐
                    │  Customer   │
                    │Requirements │
                    └─────────────┘
                           │
                    ┌─────────────┐
                    │ Feasibility │
                    │    Study    │
                    └─────────────┘

┌─────────────┐                    ┌─────────────┐
│ Preliminary │                    │Cost Request │
│Draft of Print│                   └─────────────┘
└─────────────┘

┌─────────────┐   ┌─────────────┐  ┌─────────────┐
│ Reliability │   │  Concept    │  │  Supplier   │
│   Targets   │   │  Selection  │  │  Selection  │
└─────────────┘   └─────────────┘  └─────────────┘

   Second          ◇ Design ◇
   Iteration       ◇ Review ◇
                      OK

┌─────────┐                         ┌─────────────┐
│  FMEA   │                         │ Fault Tree  │
└─────────┘                         │  Analysis   │
                                    └─────────────┘

┌─────────────┐                    ┌─────────────┐
│ Test Plans  │                    │  Qualified  │
└─────────────┘                    │ Parts List  │
                                   └─────────────┘

                   ◇ Design ◇
   Second          ◇ Review ◇
   Iteration          OK

┌─────────────┐  ┌─────────────┐  ┌─────────────┐
│Build Series A│ │Build Series B│ │Build Series C│
│ Prototypes  │  │ Prototypes  │  │ Prototypes  │
└─────────────┘  └─────────────┘  └─────────────┘

                  ┌─────────────┐
                  │ Reliability │
                  │  Analysis   │
                  └─────────────┘

   Second          ◇ Design ◇      OK    Final
   Iteration       ◇ Review ◇  ───────►  Print
                                         Approved
```

Figure 6-A

273

Failure Modes and Effects Analysis

Pareto Chart:

This chart is used to depict the root causes leading to a failure mode. Existing data on similar designs can be evaluated by using Pareto analysis to organize this data from log sheets, inspection forms, or warranty reports. The under lying message supported by the Pareto principle is that only a few of the causes identified are likely to contribute to the majority of the potential failure mode. These are referred to as root causes and should be transferred to the FMEA form. The following example demonstrates the construction of a Pareto chart using data from log sheets.

Example

A potential process failure mode was identified during the brainstorming phase of the process FMEA. The potential failure mode "rough machine finish" for this new process was predicted based on the historical failure modes experienced on similar process over the past few years. A sample of the maintenance logs and the inspection records for this operation provided the following data:

Cause A leading to "rough machine finish" occurred eight (8) times over the past three months.
Cause B 2
Cause C 23
Cause D 17
Cause E 5
Cause F 1
Cause G 2
Cause H 31
Cause J 4
                    Total 85

Step 1   Arrange the causes in descending order of frequencies. Label and place them on a horizontal
scale. For our example, the descending order is: H,
C, D, E, J, B, G, and F.

Step 2   Extend the vertical scale to the left an upward from
the horizontal scale. Label this scale from zero to
the number from cause with the highest frequency.
For our example, the number is 31.

Step 3   Construct a vertical bar for each cause on the chart.
The height of the bar is determined by the corresponding frequency of the cause. The height of the
first bar, Cause H, is 31.

Step 4   Construct a vertical scale to the right and upward
from the horizontal scale. Label the scale from zero
to one hundred percent.

Step 5   Stack up the bars of the top three or four causes and
trace a horizontal line from the pinnacle of the
stack to the scale on the right. Read the percentage
these few causes contribute to "rough machine
finish."

An example of this chart is shown in Figure 7-A.

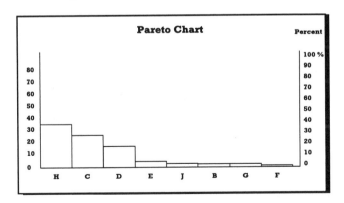

Figure 7-A

Failure Modes and Effects Analysis

FMEA Construction Tools

Input Matrix

The input matrix is a new tool introduced in the 1994 SAE paper titled "Restoring the Effectiveness of FMEA." It is designed to allow the participation of individuals that are located in separate facilities, cities, states, or countries. This matrix has proven very useful for companies that have engineering facilities and manufacturing operations located in separate states. This matrix has also proven to be more efficient and effective in both time conservation and increasing the accuracy of the information being extracted from the FMEA team.

Blank copies of this matrix (shown in Figure 8-A) are mailed to all FMEA team members along with an introductory letter and any additional design/process development support data. These input matrices are completed and returned or mailed to the designated FMEA coordinator. The coordinator feeds the information either a standard FMEA form or an FMEA Area Chart.

Failure Modes	Effects	Sev.	Cause	Occ.	Det.
1	a	#		#	
	b	#		#	
2	a	#		#	
3	a	#		#	
	b	#		#	
	c	#		#	

(X,Y) Coordinates

Figure 8-A

Fishbone Diagram:

The Fishbone diagram, also referred to as the Cause-and-Effect or Ishikawa Diagram, is used to structure causes identified in open discussions during meetings. Typically, discussions during FMEA are more spontaneous and less structured. The secretary or recorder for that FMEA meeting can construct a Fishbone diagram to organize the causes identified for each failure mode identified in the meeting. An example of the Fishbone diagram is shown in Figure 9-A.

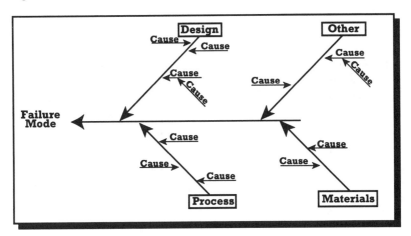

Figure 9-A

Failure Modes and Effects Analysis

Rating and Ranking Matrix:

The rating and ranking matrix has three objectives: 1) to extract the most representative rating from a team rating, 2) to identify any splits of outliers in the team ratings and 3) to identify the most important item by ranking the items in descending order. An example of the rating and ranking matrix is shown in Figure 10-A. This method proves to be more accurate than weighted voting methods and letting the person with the highest salary choose, and the rating and ranking method proves to be more cost-effective and efficient than consensus.

Failure	Effect	Cause	Detection	1	2	3	4	5	6	7	Median
	A			8	–	8	9	9	9	10	9
	B			2	7	7	7	8	9	9	OUTLIER
	C			2	2	3	3	8	8	9	SPLIT
	D			7	7	7	7	7	7	7	7

Figure 10-A

Scatter Plots:

The scatter plot is a simple graphical tool that can be used to investigate the association between a failure mode and a cause. This tool should be used when the FMEA team cannot agree or simply doesn't know if a particular cause can lead to a failure mode. Typically, "splits" or "outliers" identified in the Rating and Ranking Matrix (Figure 10-A) that cannot be resolved through team discussion can be resolved by constructing a scatter plot. A example demonstrating associations between a failure mode and a cause are shown in Figure 11-A.

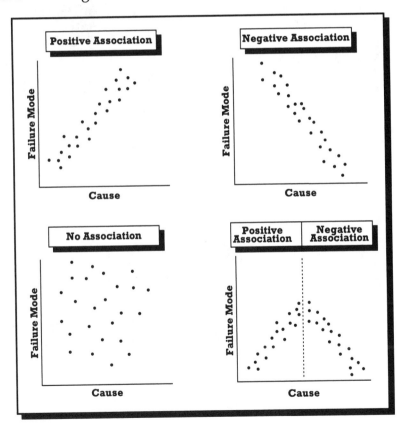

Figure 11-A

Failure Modes and Effects Analysis

FMEA Analytical Tools

Area Chart:

The Area Chart is a new development used to separate the identified failure modes into three categories: 1) High Priority, 2) Medium Priority and 3) Low Priority. The advantage this chart has over the traditional method for assessing the failure mode risk (RPN) is the Area chart assesses the failure mode using only the severity and occurrence ratings which are proactive. An example of the Area Chart is shown in Figure 12-A.

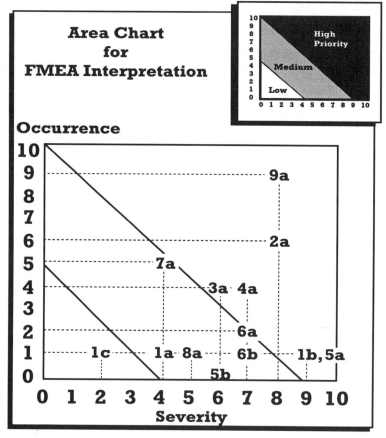

Figure 12-A

Fault Tree Analysis:

Fault tree analysis is a top-down graphical tool that provides an in-depth evaluation of a single fault or failure mode, referred to as the "top event." Fault trees can be constructed for individual failure modes identified in the FMEA that have a high severity rating or a high occurrence rating. The construction of the fault tree begins with identification of the top event. Causes leading to the top event are listed below it, then connected with lines as shown in Figure 13-A. Often these causes can be generated by more basic causes; if so, these basic causes are identified and listed below the first tier causes and connected with lines. The fault tree can have several tiers of causes ultimately leading to the top event. The logic or the way these causes combine to generate the top event can also be depicted in the fault tree. This logic can be used to predict or estimate the probability of occurrence of the failure mode or for of a cause in the FMEA.

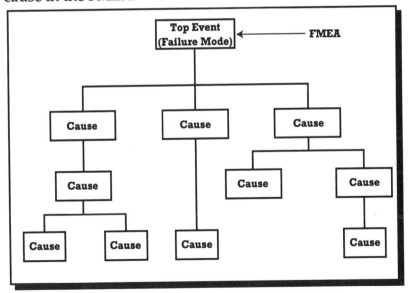

Figure 13-A

Failure Modes and Effects Analysis

Cause Screening Matrix

The Cause Screening Matrix, shown in Figure 14-A, is a new development also introduced in the 1994 SAE paper, "Restoring the Effectiveness of FMEA." This matrix highlights the causes that contribute to the majority of the high-priority failure modes identified in the FMEA and depicted in the high-priority region of the FMEA Area Chart. This strategy allows the FMEA team to "high leverage" the company's resources allocated to the design/process improvements.

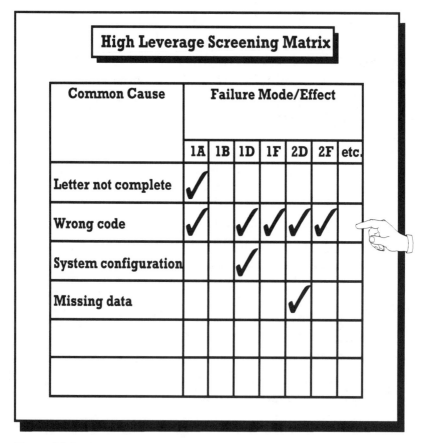

High Leverage Screening Matrix

Common Cause	Failure Mode/Effect						
	1A	1B	1D	1F	2D	2F	etc.
Letter not complete	✓						
Wrong code	✓		✓	✓	✓	✓	
System configuration			✓				
Missing data					✓		

Figure 14-A

Capability Indicators & the Standard Deviation:

Capability Indicators and the Standard Deviation are tools use to the measure the quality of the performance of the design/process. This is accomplished by taking repeated measurements of a design characteristic or a process parameter, calculating the average and the standard deviation of these measurements and comparing them to the specification. The standard deviation equals one standard unit of variation and is the most common measure of variation used in statistics. The formula for the standard deviation that applies to data that exhibits a "bell-shaped" histogram is:

$$\text{Sigma} = \frac{\text{Summation } (Xi - \overline{X})^2}{\sqrt{(n-1)}}$$

Where:
Sigma = Standard Deviation
Xi = the individual measurements
$\overline{\overline{X}}$ = the average of all the measurements
n = the total number of measurements

Capability indicators compare the design/process performance against the specification. Three common capability indicators are Cp, Cpk and Cpm:

$$Cp = \frac{(USL-LSL)}{6(\text{Sigma})} \qquad Cpk = \frac{Z \text{ minimum}}{3}$$

$$Cpm = \frac{(USL-LSL)}{6\sqrt{(\text{Sigma}^2 + (\overline{\overline{X}} - T))^2}}$$

Where:

USL = Upper Specification Limit

LSL = Lower Specification Limit

T = The Specification Target

Z = The minimum distance between the specification limits and the average calculated from the measurements. The formulas for "Z" are shown below:

$$Z \text{ (Upper Spec.)} = \frac{(USL-X)}{Sigma}$$

$$Z \text{ (Lower Spec.)} = \frac{(LSL-X)}{Sigma}$$

The first capability indicator, Cp, is simple a ratio of the variation allowed by the specification divided by the variation produced by the design/process measurements. It does not take into account the average of the measurements or the specification target. The problem with this indicator is that it is possible to calculate an acceptable Cp, although most or all of these measurements may lie outside of the specification limits!

The second capability indicator, Cpk, addresses the problem of Cp. The Cpk indicator is also a ratio of the variation allowed by the specification divided by the variation produced by the measurements. However, the Cpk formula does consider the location of the average of these measurements in relationship to the specification limits. Including the design/process average into the capability formula insures that an acceptable capability indicator can only be achieved for measurements within specification. The Cpk indicator does not take into consideration the relationship of the average of the measurements to the specification target, making it possible to calculate an acceptable Cpk value for measurements that are clustered close to one of the specifications limits and away from the specification target.

The third capability indicator, Cpm, compares the variation allowed by the specification limits to the variation in the measurements from the design/process, as well as taking into account the location of the average of these measurements to the specification target. More information on this subject is contained in the writing of Dr. Genichi Taguchi in his introduction of the "Loss Function."

Examples of the three capability indices are shown in Figure 15-A.

Distribution 1

Cp = [18-2]/6[0.707] .... = 3.77

Cpk = [5-2]/0.707 = 4.24 and 4.24/3 .... = 1.40

Cpm = [18-2]/6[0.707^2 + (5-1-)^2]$^{0.5}$ .... = 0.53

Distribution 2

Cp = [18-2]/6[1.633] .... = 1.63

Cpk = [18-20]/1.633 = 1.22 and 1.22/3 .... = 0.40

Cpm = [18-2]/6[1.633^2 + (20-10-)^2]$^{0.5}$ .... = 0.26

Distribution 3

Cp = [18-2]/6[2.45] .... = 1.09

Cpk = [10-18/2.45 = 3.26 and 3.26/3 .... = 1.09

Cpm = [18-2]/1[2.45^2 + (10-10)^2]$^{0.5}$ .... = 1.09

Failure Modes and Effects Analysis

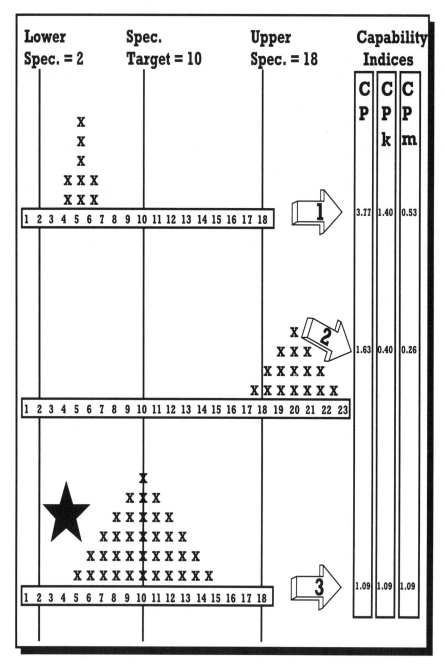

Figure 15-A

Appendix C:
Case Study

FMEA Case Study

The following FMEA case study was completed on a recently introduced electric hair dryer. The FMEA was part of an overall QFD (Quality Function Deployment) project which served as reference for the FMEA to aid in the identification of additional expected functions and subsequent potential failure modes. *This FMEA was preformed over a four month period by a team of graduate engineers, coordinated by Mr. Muhammad Sohail Ahmed, from the College of Engineering, Department of Manufacturing and Industrial Engineering Wayne State University, Detroit, Michigan.*

Introduction:

A new medium class hair dryer has been recently introduced. The first quarterly sale figures on this new design were far below the projected sales forecast. The design team elected to conduct an independent study to investigate this design and to try and determine the root causes of this problem.

FMEA Planning:

The team began by developing a Gantt timing chart (shown in Figure 1), along with a Roles and Responsibilities matrix (shown in Figure 2), to help facilitate this project. A customer profile was generated for this design and used to conducted surveys for developing a list of customer expectations or customer wants. This information was used to help in the identification of the design functions for the FMEA. Once the customer expectations were translated into design requirements using the first phase of Quality Function Deployment, the team developed the design operating/environmental profiles (shown in Figure 3 & 4). The next task in the planning of the FMEA was the completion of a Concept Selection study (shown in Figure 5). The new hair dryer baseline, was compared against other comparable hair dryer designs to assess which of these designs could best satisfy the customers expectation and the design requirements. A block diagram (shown in Figure 6) was then developed for the chosen concept prior to the construction of the FMEA to assist the team in understanding the functional relationship of the design subsystems and components.

FMEA Construction:

The design FMEA was divided into nine individual subsystem and component FMEAs:

1. Casting FMEA
2. Circuit Breaker FMEA
3. Stationary Vanes FMEA
4. Fan/Rotor Assembly FMEA
5. Electric Cord FMEA
6. Circuit Breaker & Cord FMEA
7. On/Off Switch FMEA
8. Motor FMEA
9. Heating Element FMEA

Fault Trees (shown in Figures 7 & 8) were constructed on two of the top failure modes identified. They were used for making the recommendations. Revisions for the On/Off Switch, the Motor ,and the Heating Element FMEAs reflect some of these recommendations along with other recommendations. These revisions are include in this case study. Each of these revisions are arranged sequentially in the revision section behind the initial FMEAs and Fault Trees.

Gantt Timing Chart

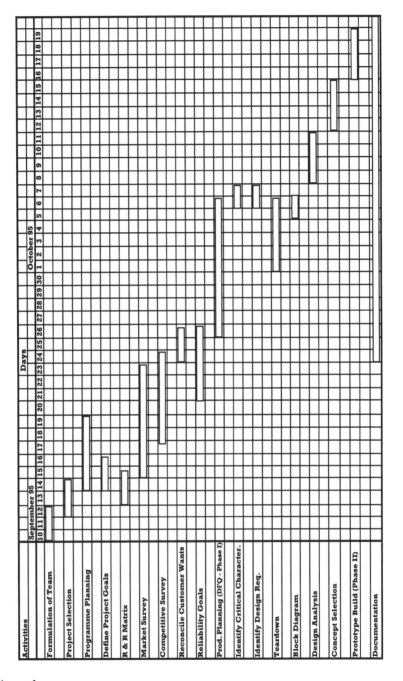

Figure 1

R & R Matrix	Design Control	Design Development
Product Engr. (Sohail Mukhtar)	• Develop Block Diagram • Assist in developing Rel. Targets • Review Supplier Reliability • Incorporate Rel. Spec.	• Incorporate Reliability Requirements into DV/PV program • Review reliability requirements
Purch. (Razzak)	• Evaluate supplier's reliability program	• Review Preliminary Module for Reliability Requirements
Supplier (Bandara)	• Reliability Program Plan • Reliability Specification • Reliability Targets	• Update Product Eng'ring • FMEA, Test Plan
Reliability Engr. (Shah Asif)	• Provide support to engineer	• Support Product Eng'ring for Reliability Analysis • Initiate and maintain Reliability Growth Curve
Supplier Quality Engr. (SAMEEM)	• Assess the Supplier's Reliability	• Review Supplier's Reliability for Mfg. program • Coordinate supplier reliability activities
Advanced Planning (Naseer)	• Identify Customer Requirements • Other Design Requirements	

Figure 2

Operational Requirements Worksheet

System: Blow Hair Dryer

Purpose/Intended Use:

Blow Dry Hair

Operational Profile:

High Temperature, Noise, Vibration

Stress	Categories	Criteria
Operating Time	40 min. (Max.) Max. 10 minutes in a stretch	Intermitent use with a break of 15 sec.
Uses per Year 365 days 15 min./use	Low Use: 1095/yr Medium Use: 1825/yr High Use: 3650/yr	Low: 3 uses/day Medium: 5 uses/day High: 10 uses/day Average: 15 uses/day
Duty Cycle	3 minutes	
Load During Operation	Gentle Dry – Low Speed (2-4) 5 inches away Curl Set – Cold Blow	
Speed During Operation	Quick Dry – High Speed (9-10) 4 inches away Soft Long Hair – Med. Speed (4-7) Thick Hair – High Speed	
Other		

Figure 3

Environmental Profile Worksheet

Environment	User	Manufacture/Inventory	Shipping
High temperature	115 F	120 F	120 F
Low temperature	-10 F	-40 F	-40 F
High relative humidity	100	100	100
Low relative humidity	10	10	10
Sand and dust	Medium	High	High
Rain	No	Medium	High
Temperature shock	50	60	70
High speed particles	No	No	Yes
Vibration	No	No	Yes
Magnetic fields	Medium	High	High
Moist and mist	High	Medium	High
Stacking limit	1+1	20/20	20/10

Figure 4

Concept Selection

CUSTOMER REQUIREMENTS	RATING	BASE LINE	NEW DESIGN	MODIFICATION #1
Electric Shock Proof	9		1	0
Light Weight	7		1	0
Longer Switch Life	9		1	1
Compact	8		0	0
Better Grip	7		0	0
# of Attachments	6		0	1
Energy Efficient	9		1	1
Removable Cord	4		0	1
Automatic Shut Off	5		0	1
TOTAL			34	33

NB: Base Line is the current standing of the company. Zero means same.

Figure 5

295

Failure Modes and Effects Analysis

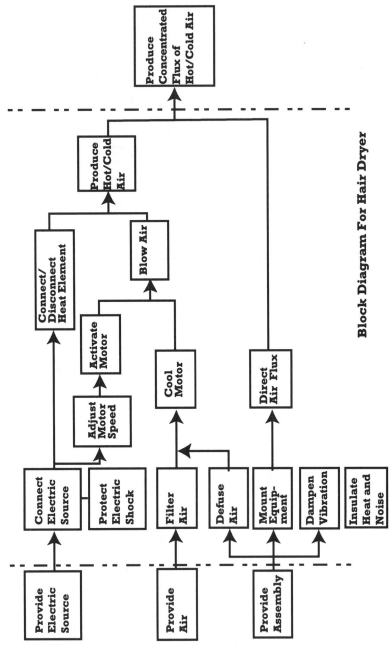

Block Diagram For Hair Dryer

Figure 6

Part/Components __Casing__
Model Year __1994__
Schedule Product Release __Dec. 07, 1994__
Outside Supplier Effected __Yes____ No _X_

Subsystem Engineer __Sohail Naseer__
System Engineer __Sameem__
FMEA Date: Original __Nov. 06, 1994__ Revised ___

ID Code	Name Number	Function	Failure Mode	Effect	SEV	OCC	Cause	DET	RPN	Recommendations	Status
C01	Casing	• To hold the components	1. Casing breaks	• Burns hand	7	1	• Mishandling physical shock	1	7		
		• Provide insulation		• Component dislocated	5	1	• Inferior quality material	1			
		• Guide air		• Customer dissatisfaction	3	1					
		• Give impressive look									

Approvals:

Design Manager __M. Sohail__
Reliability Supervisor __S. Asif__

Concurrence:

Staff Quality Control _____
Plant Quality Control _____

NOTE – DET: Detection, RPN: Risk Priority Number, OCC: Occurrence, SEV: Severity

Failure Modes and Effects Analysis

Part/ Components __Circuit Breaker__

Model Year __1994__

Schedule Product Release __Dec. 06, 1994__

Outside Supplier Effected Yes __X__ No___

Subsystem Engineer __Muktar__

System Engineer __Razaq__

FMEA Date: Original __Nov. 06, 1994__ Revised ___

ID Code	Name Number	Function	Failure Mode	Effect	SEV	OCC	Cause	DET	RPN	Recommendations	Status
S07	Circuit Breaker	To disconnect electric power in case of short circuit	Solonide relay damaged	Electric shock	10	1	• Bad relay • Overheating	7	70		

Approvals:

Design Manager __M. Sohail Ahmed__

Reliability Supervisor __S. Asif Ali__

Concurrence:

Staff Quality Control ___

Plant Quality Control ___

NOTE – DET: Detection, RPN: Risk Priority Number, OCC: Occurrence, SEV: Severity

Part/Components **Stationary Vanes**

Model Year **1994**

Schedule Product Release **Dec. 07, 1994**

Outside Supplier Effected Yes **X** No

Subsystem Engineer **Sohail Naseer**

System Engineer **Sameem**

FMEA Date: Original **Nov. 06, 1994 Revised**

ID Code	Name Number	Function	Failure Mode	Effect	SEV	O C C	Cause	D E T	R P N	Recommendations	Status
C02	Stationary Vanes	• Increase pressure and velocity head of air • Guide air	1. Vane breaks	• Reduced throw of air • Undesirable air path	5	3	• Physical shock	3	45		

Approvals:

Design Manager **M. Sohail**

Reliability Supervisor **S. Asif**

Concurrence:

Staff Quality Control

Plant Quality Control

NOTE – DET: Detection, RPN: Risk Priority Number, OCC: Occurrence, SEV: Severity

Failure Modes and Effects Analysis

Part/ Components Fan/Rotor Assembly
Model Year 1994
Schedule Product Release Dec. 07, 1994
Outside Supplier Effected Yes _____ No _X_

Subsystem Engineer Hisham
System Engineer Neelanganie
FMEA Date: Original Nov. 06, 1994 Revised _____

ID Code	Name Number	Function	Failure Mode	Effect	SEV	OCC	Cause	DET	RPN	Recommendations	Status
C03	Rotor	Suck and blow air	1. Rotor vanes break	Reduced air flow	5	2	• Physical shock • Mishandling • Inferior material	1	10	Upgrade material	

Approvals:

Design Manager M. Sohail
Reliability Supervisor S. Asif

Concurrence:

Staff Quality Control _____
Plant Quality Control _____

NOTE – DET: Detection, RPN: Risk Priority Number, OCC: Occurrence, SEV: Severity

Part/ Components __Electrical Cord__
Model Year __1994__
Schedule Product Release __Dec. 06, 1994__
Outside Supplier Effected Yes __X__ No __

Subsystem Engineer __Muktar__
System Engineer __Neelanganie__
FMEA Date: Original __Nov. 06, 1994 Revised__

ID Code Number	Name	Function	Failure Mode	Effect	SEV	O C C	Cause	D E T	R P N	Recommendations	Status
S04	Electrical Cord	To carry current	1. Cord cut	• Electrical shock • Dryer won't work	8	1	Mishandling	1	8	• Better material with high moldability should be used	In process
			2. Cord burn	• Electrical shock • Dryer won't work	8	1		1	8	• Check and revise the spec. to incorporate electrical power • Over design the cord	

Approvals:

Design Manager __M. Sohail Ahmed__
Reliability Supervisor __S. Asif Ali__

Concurrence:

Staff Quality Control _____
Plant Quality Control _____

NOTE – DET: Detection, RPN: Risk Priority Number, OCC: Occurrence, SEV: Severity

Failure Modes and Effects Analysis

Part/ Components Circuit Breaker & Cord
Model Year 1994
Schedule Product Release Dec. 06, 1994
Outside Supplier Effected Yes___ X___ No___

Subsystem Engineer Hasham
System Engineer Sameem
FMEA Date: Original Nov. 06, 1994 Revised___

ID Code	Name Number	Function	Failure Mode	Effect	SEV	O C C	Cause	D E T	R P N	Recommendations	Status
SS01	Circuit breaker subassembly	To supply electric power and disconnect in case of short circuit	1. Cord burns	• Electrical shock	9	1	• Overheat	5	45		In process
				• No electric supply	7	1	• Mishandling	5	35	Redesign the inspection	
			2. Cord cut		7	1	• Inferior material of cord	4	28		
			3. Relay malfunction								

Approvals:

Design Manager Muhammad Sohail Ahmed
Reliability Supervisor Syed Asif Ali

Concurrence:

Staff Quality Control _____
Plant Quality Control _____

NOTE – DET: Detection, RPN: Risk Priority Number, OCC: Occurrence, SEV: Severity

Part/ Components ___On/Off Switch___
Model Year ___1994___
Schedule Product Release ___Dec. 06, 1994___
Outside Supplier Effected Yes___X___ No___

Subsystem Engineer ___S. Muktar___
System Engineer ___A. Razaq___
FMEA Date: Original ___Nov. 06, 1994___ Revised ___

ID Code	Name Number	Function	Failure Mode	Effect	SEV	OCC	Cause	DET	RPN	Recommendations	Status
S02	On/off switch	To start and stop the hair dryer opreation	1. Switch spring broken	• No hot/cold air	7	3	• Physicl shock • Fatigue	9	189	Reconfirm switch spec. Redesign, if necessary	In process
			2. Contact point burned	• No hot/cold air	7	3	• Loose contact	7	147	Inspect switches at supplier's workplace to confirm spec.	

Approvals:

Design Manager ___Muhammad Sohail Ahmed___
Reliability Supervisor ___Syed Asif Ali___

Concurrence:

Staff Quality Control ___
Plant Quality Control ___

NOTE – DET: Detection, RPN: Risk Priority Number, OCC: Occurrence, SEV: Severity

303

Failure Modes and Effects Analysis

Part/Components __Motor__
Model Year __1994__
Schedule Product Release __Dec. 06, 1994__
Outside Supplier Effected Yes __X__ No ____

Subsystem Engineer __S. Muktar__
System Engineer __A. Razaq__
FMEA Date: Original __Nov. 06, 1994__ Revised ____

ID Code	Name Number	Function	Failure Mode	Effect	SEV	OCC	Cause	DET	RPN	Recommendations	Status
S01	Motor	To drive the rotor	1. Seizure of the shaft	• Overheat the motor • Cord burns • Motor winding burns • Rotor stops	7	9	• Insufficient lubrication	2	126	Modify lubrication process or use better lubricant	
			2. Motor burns				• Overload • Overheat • Winding insulation damage				

Approvals:

Design Manager __M. Sohail Ahmed__
Reliability Supervisor __S. Asif Ali__

Concurrence:

Staff Quality Control ____
Plant Quality Control ____

NOTE – DET: Detection, RPN: Risk Priority Number, OCC: Occurrence, SEV: Severity

Appendix C

Part/Components __Heating Element & Potentiometer__
Model Year __1994__
Schedule Product Release __Dec. 06, 1994__
Outside Supplier Effected Yes __X__ No ___

Subsystem Engineer __Hisham__
System Engineer __Sameem__
FMEA Date: Original __Nov. 07, 1994__ Revised ___

ID Code	Name Number	Function	Failure Mode	Effect	SEV	OCC	Cause	DET	RPN	Recommendations	Status
S05	Heating Element	To heat air	1. Element broken	No hot air	4	3	• Physical shock • Overheat	1	12		
S06	Potentio-meter	To vary temp-erature and air throw	1. Potentio-meter fails	Constant temperature and air throw	5	5	• Overload • Longer operation time	5	125	Swap	In process

Approvals:

Design Manager __M. Sohail Ahmed__
Reliability Supervisor __S. Asif Ali Shah__

Concurrence:

Staff Quality Control ___
Plant Quality Control ___

NOTE – DET: Detection, RPN: Risk Priority Number, OCC: Occurrence, SEV: Severity

305

Failure Modes and Effects Analysis

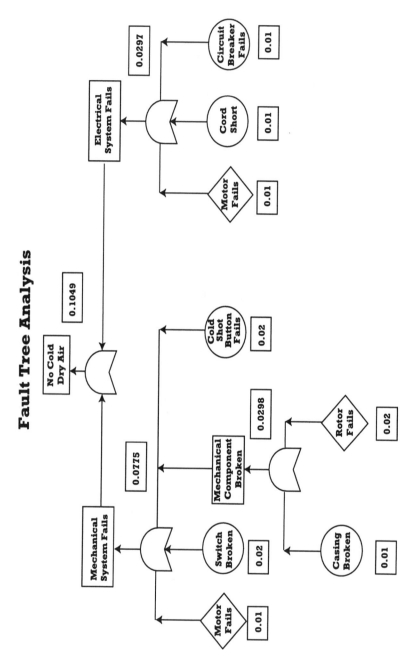

Figure 7

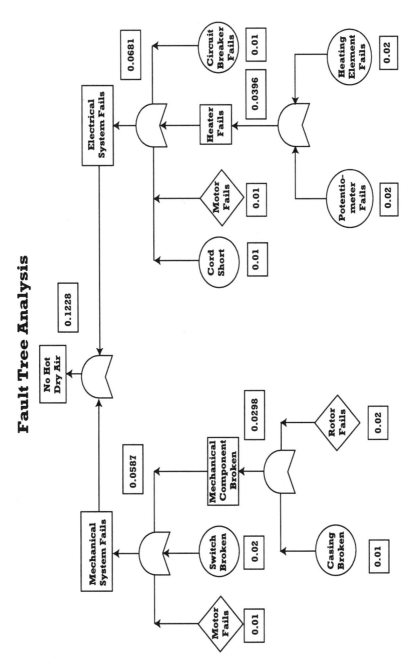

Figure 8

Failure Modes and Effects Analysis

Part/Components __On/Off Switch__
Model Year __1994__
Schedule Product Release __Dec. 06, 1994__
Outside Supplier Effected Yes __X__ No____

Subsystem Engineer __S. Muktar__
System Engineer __A. Razaq__
FMEA Date: Original __Nov. 06, 1994__ Revised __Nov. 16, 1994__

ID Code	Name Number	Function	Failure Mode	Effect	SEV	OCC	Cause	DET	RPN	Recommendations	Status
S02	On/off switch	To start and stop the hair dryer opreation	1. Switch spring broken	• No hot/cold air	7	1	• Physicl shock • Fatigue	3	21		Completed on Nov. 15, 1994
			2. Contact point burned	• No hot/cold air	7	3	• Loose contact	7	147	Inspect switches at supplier's workplace to confirm spec.	In process

Approvals:

Design Manager __M. Sohail Ahmed__
Reliability Supervisor __S. Asif Ali__

Concurrence:

Staff Quality Control ____
Plant Quality Control ____

NOTE – DET: Detection, RPN: Risk Priority Number, OCC: Occurrence, SEV: Severity

Part/Components: __On/Off Switch__
Model Year: __1994__
Schedule Product Release: __Dec. 06, 1994__
Outside Supplier Effected Yes __X__ No ____

Subsystem Engineer: __S. Muktar__
System Engineer: __A. Razaq__
FMEA Date: Original __Nov. 06, 1994__ Revised __Nov. 20, 1994__

ID Code	Name Number	Function	Failure Mode	Effect	SEV	OCC	Cause	DET	RPN	Recommendations	Status
S02	On/off switch	To start and stop the hair dryer operation	1. Switch spring broken	• No hot/cold air	7	1	• Physical shock • Fatigue	3	21		
			2. Contact point burned	• No hot/cold air	7	1	• Loose contact	7	49		Completed on Nov. 19, 1994

Approvals:

Design Manager: __M. Sohail Ahmed__
Reliability Supervisor: __S. Asif Ali__

Concurrence:

Staff Quality Control ____
Plant Quality Control ____

NOTE – DET: Detection, RPN: Risk Priority Number, OCC: Occurrence, SEV: Severity

Failure Modes and Effects Analysis

Part/ Components __Motor__

Model Year __1994__

Schedule Product Release __Dec. 06, 1994__

Outside Supplier Effected Yes __X__ No __

Subsystem Engineer __S. Muktar__

System Engineer __A. Razaq__

FMEA Date: Original __Nov. 06, 1994__ Revised __Nov. 16, 1994__

ID Code	Name Number	Function	Failure Mode	Effect	SEV	O C C	Cause	D E T	R P N	Recommendations	Status
S01	Motor	To drive the rotor	1. Seizure of the shaft	• Overheat the motor • Cord burns • Motor winding burns • Rotor stops	7	9	• Insufficient lubrication	2	42		Recommendations completed on Nov. 15, 1994
			2. Motor burns				• Overload • Overheat • Winding insulation damage				

Approvals:

Design Manager __M. Sohail Ahmed__

Reliability Supervisor __S. Asif Ali__

Concurrence:

Staff Quality Control _____

Plant Quality Control _____

NOTE – DET: Detection, RPN: Risk Priority Number, OCC: Occurrence, SEV: Severity

310

Part / Components Heating Element & Potentiometer
Model Year 1994
Schedule Product Release Dec. 06, 1994
Outside Supplier Effected Yes __X__ No ____

Subsystem Engineer Hisham
System Engineer Sameem
FMEA Date: Original Nov. 07, 1994 Revised Nov. 16, 1994

ID Code	Name Number	Function	Failure Mode	Effect	SEV	O C C	Cause	D E T	R P N	Recommendations	Status
S05	Heating Element	To heat air	1. Element broken	No hot air	4	3	• Physical shock • Overheat	1	12		
S06	Potentio-meter	To vary the temperature and air throw	1. Potentio-meter fails	Constant temperature and air throw	5	3	• Overload • Longer operation time	5	75	Use higher power potentiometer	In process

Approvals:

Design Manager M. Sohail Ahmed
Reliability Supervisor S. Asif Ali Shah

Concurrence:

Staff Quality Control _____
Plant Quality Control _____

NOTE – DET: Detection, RPN: Risk Priority Number, OCC: Occurrence, SEV: Severity

Failure Modes and Effects Analysis

Part/ Components Heating Element & Potentiometer
Model Year 1994
Schedule Product Release Dec. 06, 1994
Outside Supplier Effected Yes X No

Subsystem Engineer Hisham
System Engineer Sameem
FMEA Date: Original Nov. 07, 1994 Revised Nov. 20, 1994

ID Code	Name Number	Function	Failure Mode	Effect	SEV	OCC	Cause	DET	RPN	Recommendations	Status
S05	Heating Element	To heat air	1. Element broken	No hot air	4	3	• Physical shock • Overheat	1	12		
S06	Potentio-meter	To vary the temperature and air throw	1. Potentio-meter fails	Constant temperature and air throw	5	1	• Overload • Longer operation time	5	25		Recommend-ations completed on Nov. 20, 1994

Approvals:

Design Manager M. Sohail Ahmed
Reliability Supervisor S. Asif Ali Shah.

Concurrence:

Staff Quality Control
Plant Quality Control

NOTE – DET: Detection, RPN: Risk Priority Number, OCC: Occurrence, SEV: Severity

"Analysis Techniques for System Reliability – Procedure for Failure Mode and Effects Analysis (FMEA)," *International Electrotechnical Commission: IEC Standard Pub. 812.* 1985

Barbour, G.L. "Failure Modes and Effects Analysis by the Matrix Method," *Proc. Ann. Reliability & Maintainability Symp.* 1977, pp 114-119.

Bajaria, Hans J. and Richard P. Copp. *Statistical Problem Solving.* Multiface Publishing Company, Garden City, MI. 1991.

Coutinho, J. S. "Failure-Effect Analysis," *Trans. New York Academy of Sciences.* 1964, pp. 564-585.

"Electronic Reliability Design Handbook," *Mil Hdbk-338-1A, Volume 1.* October 12, 1993.

"Failure Mode and Effect Analyses," *Electronic Industries Association G-41 Committee on Reliability: Reliability Bulletin No 9.* November 1971.

Failure Mode, Effects, and Criticality Analysis (FMECA). CRTA-FMECA Reliability Analysis Center, Rome, NY. 1993.

"Failure Mode/Mechanism Distributions 1991," *FMD-91,* Reliability Analysis Center. 1991.

"Fault/Failure Analysis Procedure," *Society of Automotive Engineers Aerospace Recommended Practice: ARP 926A.* November 15, 1979.

"The FMECA Process in the Concurrent Engineering (CE) Environment," *Society of Automotive Engineers Aerospace Information Report: AIR 4845.* June 18, 1993.

Failure Modes and Effects Analysis

Palady, P., M. Horvath, and C. Thomas. "Restoring the Effectiveness of Failure Modes and Effects Analysis." Society of Automotive Engineers Technical Paper 940884.

"Potential Failure Modes and Effects Analysis in Design (Design FMEA) and For Manufacturing and Assembly Processes (Process FMEA) Reference Manual." *Society of Automotive Engineers, Surface Vehicle Recommended Practice: J1739.* November 15, 1979.

"Procedures for Performing a Failure Mode Effects and Criticality Analysis." *US Mil-Std.-1629-A/Notice 2.* November 15, 1984.

"Reliability Prediction of Electronic Equipment." *Mil-Hndbk-217F/Notice 2.* December 10, 1993.

area chart...................... One of the new developments that enables a proactive interpretation of FMEA from the plotted coordinates of the severity rating and the occurrence rating of the failure mode or cause.

appraisal cost .... The cost incurred from audits and planned inspection to assure that the quality system is in place and indeed working.

attribute data................ Data that cannot be measure on a continuous scale. Examples include good/bad, low/medium/high and other type of truncated classifications.

benchmarking.............. An analysis or comparison of the competition's quality. The highest quality of a particular design is often referred to as the "benchmark."

BIT (Built-in-test)........ Self-inspection or diagnostic equipment that is designed into the product to provide an ongoing status of the design quality.

block diagram .... A picture of the design or subsystem represented by a collection of rectangles arranged to represent the logic of the design.

bottom-up FMEA .... An approach for developing an FMEA starting with the individual components and finishing with the complete system.

brainstorming .... A strategy or procedure for generating ideas or clues to a problem or a project.

capability indicators ... Ratios of the design variation compared against the process variation.

cGMP .... Current Good Manufacturing Practices. A series of quality standards from the FDA's (Food and Drug Administration) guidelines for quality systems.

concept selection .... A technique for selecting the best design, process or service concept base on how each concept satisfies all the requirements identified.

contingency table analysis .... CTA. A statistical technique used to make comparisons between groups of attribute data.

control characteristic .. Anything that can be measured to assess the quality or reliability of a design that is very important to the final quality and reliability of that design.

control upstream .... A strategy for controlling the quality and the reliability upstream in the overall development process. Often refers to designing-in features that ensure the quality and reliability.

control plan .... A document that provides the outline or strategy of all the actions required during the actual manufacturing or processing to assure the final quality targets.

control point (design) Features or characteristics of the design or design process that have been designated for evaluating and controlling the overall quality/program targets.

control point (process) Features or parameters of the process that have been designated for evaluation and control to ensure the manufacturing quality.

correlation .... A measure of the association, *not relationships*, between a failure mode and a cause or any other two items.

criticality number ...... Cr. A statistic used to measure the importance of a failure mode when preforming FMECA. As specified in the Military Standard 1629A of the Department of Defense (DOD).

DDDR .... Detail Detail Design Review. A formal review of the final design to assure that all design issues have been resolved and that the design is ready for approval and subsequent prototype build.

detection (sense 1) .... Measured using a rating number, it is a measure of how effective, the method of detection is in preventing a problem from reaching the customers. This definition of detection applies to the Detection column in the FMEA.

detection (sense 2) .... Design actions of how the customer will be able to detect and avoid a catastrophic failure before it occurs. Detection for the customer during use.

DFMEA .... Design Failure Modes and Effects Analysis.

DOE .... Design of Experiments. Planned statistical studies to quantify the contribution that each variable contributes to a problem and to identify the best adjustment of the most significant contributors to achieve a desired outcome or minimize the problem.

ES .... Engineering Specification.

failure cost .... The cost initiated by a failure.

fault hazard analysis .. See FMEA.

FDA .... Food and Drug Administration.

find-and-fix .... A reactive strategy for identifying problems for resolution.

FMEA .... Failure Modes and Effects Analysis. A technique for preventing problems during the design development process. FMEA serves a diary of the design, process or service being provided.

FMECA .... Failure Modes, Effects and Criticality Analysis. See FMEA.

forgiving principle ..... A strategy for forgiving or compensating quality problems downstream in the process or during customer use.

FPDR .... Final Production Design Review. A formal review to assure that the design is ready to launch and that all the process/manufacturing issues have been resolved.

FTA .... Fault Tree Analysis. A technique for depicting all the possible ways a fault or problem can be created. FTA can also be used to assist in estimating the failure rate of the fault based in the historical quality of the causes leading to the fault.

hazard analysis .... See FMEA.

ID .... Inside Diameter.

input form (FMEA) ..... A new development of FMEA that is used to collect data more efficiently and cost effectively to construct the FMEA form.

ISO 9000 .... The International Organization of "Quality Series" Standards/Guidelines for quality systems.

linkage (FMEA) .... Refers to quality and reliability techniques that are used to support the construction of FMEA and to perform the analysis of FMEA. Also refers to documents within the organization that influence or are influenced by the FMEA.

loss function................. A concept/technique introduced by Dr. G. Taguchi to conduct cost/benefit studies using the total cost.

manufacturing control plan .... See Control Plan.

Mil-Std 1629A .... A standard for developing FMEA suggested by the Department of Defense.

observational study .... The collection of data via passive observation and recording. This data is then analyzed using one of the design of experiments for decision making.

OD................................ Outside Diameter.

OEM .... Original Equipment Manufacturer.

outlier .... Data that may be representative of the subject matter under study; however, distinctly apart (much higher or lower) than the rest of the data collected.

pareto diagram............ A picture drawn from collected data that uses bar charts to depict the contribution that each variable adds to the overall problem or area of interest. The underlying concepts is that a few of these variable will contribute to the majority of the problem or area of interest, roughly 80/20.

PCDR........................... Preliminary Concept Design Review. A formal review to determine if the best concept has been selected and that all the preliminary project planning issues have been resolved before proceeding with the design or the process planning.

permanency.................. The concept of how effective a solution is and how permanent the solution will be adhered to.

PFD .... Process Flow Diagram.

PFMEA .... Process Failure Modes and Effects Analysis.

PM .... Preventative Maintenance.

PPM

(Parts Per Million) ...... A statistic sometimes use to measure the quality level of a design. For example, 90 PPM can be restated as: ninety parts per million parts.

prevention cost .... All expenditures allocated to activities for planning and preventing problems.

proactive .... Anticipating and resolving problems before they actually occur.

process map .... A flow chart depicting all the program/project tasks and the relationship of these task.**pugh matrix** See Concept Selection.

QFD .... Quality Function Deployment. A technique for capturing the "voice of the customer" and using this voice to guide the design development, the process development and the actual manufacturing operation.

QS-9000
Quality Standard......... The new joint quality standard for Chrysler, Ford and General Motors.

quality contract............ A detailed description listing the control characteristics and the means of assuring the quality and reliability of these characteristics. This contract is binding and usually appended to the purchasing agreement.

rating and ranking
matrix/guide .... Used to structure and analyze all the subjective voting of team members to identify the most representative team vote.

reactive .... The strategy of observing an actual problem and then attempting to resolve this problem. Similar to "find-and-fix."

redundant system .... A design that used a backup system, standby or active, to reduce the occurrence of a failure mode or to increase the operating time of the design.

roles and responsibility matrix/guide .... Used to define everyone's role and responsibility for a project.

robust design .... Refers to the strategy of designing such that the design is insensitive to uncontrolled variation that will affect the design's quality performance.

root cause .... The cause that exerts the most influence on the problem or area under study.

RPN............................... Risk Priority Number. The traditional approach for interpreting FMEA, which includes reactive elements.

SCR .... Service Call Rate. A statistic used by some organizations to measure the quality of a design by tracking the number of service call required to repair a design over a fixed amount of time.

series A prototype .... Often refers to one or two prototypes built and tested to demonstrate function only.

series B prototype .... A limited number of prototypes built and tested to demonstrate durability requirements only.

series C prototype .... Larger numbers of prototypes built and tested to demonstrate quality and reliability targets established for the overall development program.

series system .... A system which has all of its components in series such that if one of these components fail the system would cease to function.

SOP .... Standard Operating Procedures. Detailed step-by-step instructions for performing a specific manufacturing or process operation/task.

SPC .... Statistical Process Control.

splits .... Slang used to describe a situation where approximately half the team rates an item low and approximately half the team rates the item high. A split would be highlighted in the R&R Matrix and assigned for further investigation.

SPS .... Statistical Problem Solving.

tolerance stack-up .... The addition of all the individual component tolerance or the tolerance of mating parts to determine the overall assembled tolerance. For example, the sum of each individual component tolerance in a retractable ball point pen (the roller ball, ink cartridge, spring and push cap) must not exceed the overall body tolerance of the pen. Note: This is not true for statistical tolerancing stack-ups.

top-down FMEA .... Constructing the system FMEA first, then constructing the subsystems FMEA and lastly, constructing the individual component FMEA.

test plan.......................... A detailed strategy for testing and evaluating the prototypes. The test plan includes: a description of the test to be preformed, the test conditions or environment, the sample size, acceptance criteria, special considerations, and a column to record the test results.

variable data................. Data that can be measured on a continuous scale, such as the diameter of a piston using a micrometer, the weight of material using a scale, the speed of an actuator, or the reaction time of a catalyst using a stop watch.

FAILURE MODES AND EFFECTS ANALYSIS SEMINARS

To begin addressing increasing complexity to interrelationships required by manufacturers to make products correctly the first time. The challenge is adoption of a failure modes and effects analysis program that uncovers many of the undesirable hazards to a process or product before beginning production and the effect it has on cost, safety, durability, and reliability.

TOPICS INCLUDE

◊ Understanding FMEA

◊ Designing and Developing More Effectively at the Start

◊ Design Analysis

◊ Developing Standardization

◊ Data Analysis – Documentation

◊ Total Cost Analysis

◊ Developing High Power Performance Teams

◊ Implementation Benefits

CALL TOLL FREE FOR MORE INFORMATION
1-800-272-4335

Subject "QUICK" Index